BASED ON *A* TRUE STORY:

Dr. John R. Adolph

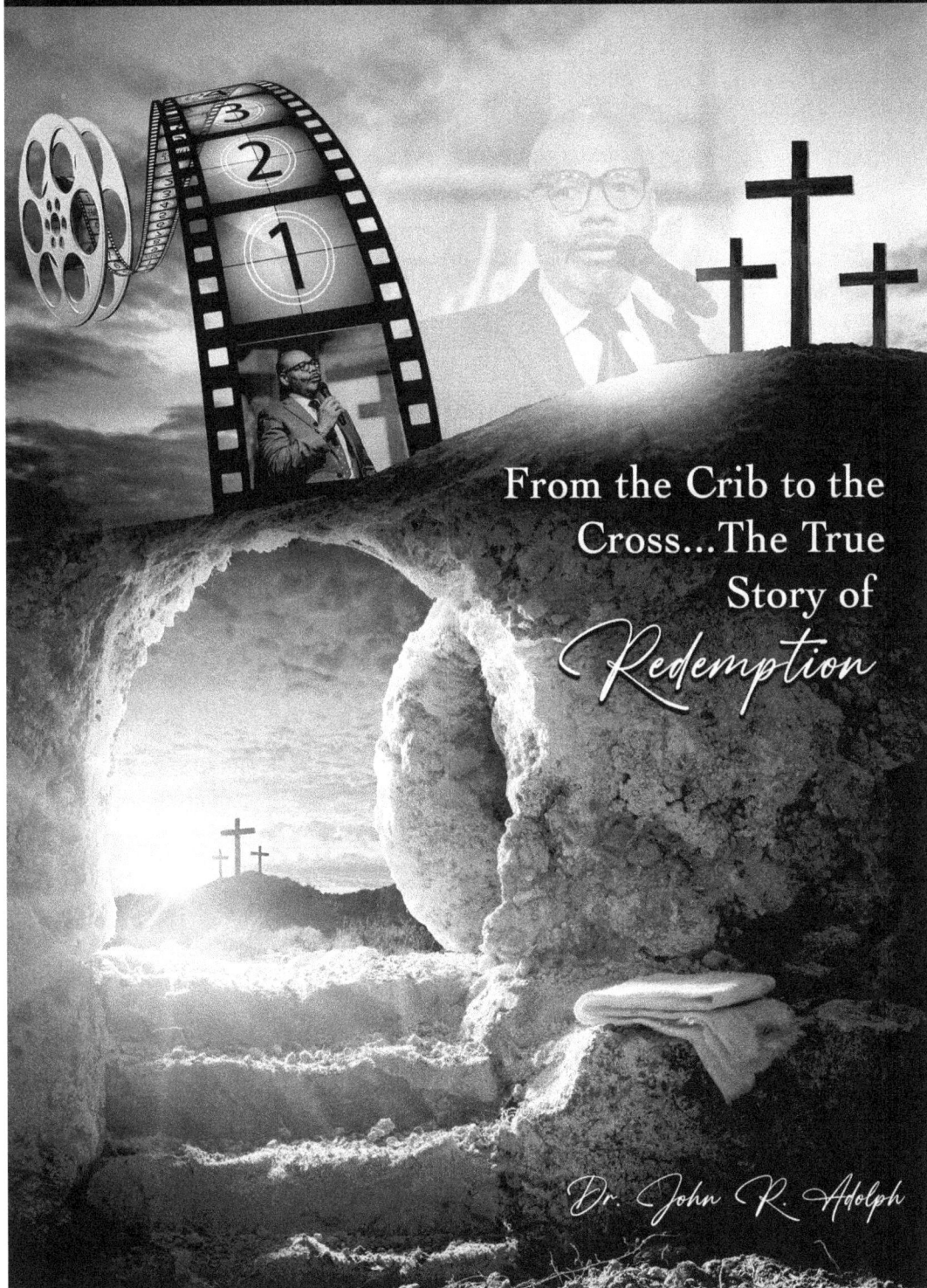

Based on a True Story: From the Crib to the Cross, The true Story of Redemption
by Dr. John R. Adolph
Copyright © 2023 by John R. Adolph
All Rights Reserved.
ISBN: 978-1-59755-770-2

Published by: ADVANTAGE BOOKS™, Orlando, FL
www.advbookstore.com

Scriptures quotations taken from the Holy Bible KING JAMES VERSION (KJV), public domain.

Library of Congress Catalog Number: 2023951260	
Name:	Adolph, John R., Author
Title:	*Based on a True Story: From the Crib to the Cross, The true Story of Redemption*
	John R. Adolph
	Advantage Books, 2023
Identifiers:	ISBN Paperback: 978159757702
	ISBN eBook: 978159757788
Subjects:	Books › Religion & Spirituality › Worship & Devotion Devotionals
	Books › Religion & Spirituality › Worship & Devotion Inspirational
	Books › Religion & Spirituality › Worship & Devotion Prayer

First Printing: December 2023
23 24 25 26 27 28   10 9 8 7 6 5 4 3 2 1

Dedication

I was raised and reared in the church. My father was my Pastor Daddy, Seymour V. Adolph Senior. My mother was a church musician who could make the melody from a piano charm the soul. I was baptized at the tender age of seven and again at eighteen years old because I wanted to commit my life to Jesus Christ as a young adult. With this at heart, make no mistake about it, I love the Lord. However, by the age of twenty-one, I left the church. You see, I was frustrated, agitated, and irritated by the continuous flaws I noticed in my life. I mean, when I thought I was sin-free and finished with making mistakes; I would see more sins and issues causing me to feel horrible. It was as if I was in a dark pit with no hope of ever getting out.

I spoke with my Father one day; I told him of my decision to leave the church. That day, my father told me something that led me to preach the Gospel of Jesus Christ to thousands worldwide. He said, "Bobby, you think too much of yourself and not enough of the finished work of Jesus Christ at the Cross. You have heard the stories of the Bible about the birth and death of Jesus. You are old enough now to go and study them. Study and you might change your mind about leaving the church. After all, why leave God, if God has never left you?"

This moment fueled a journey setting the course of my life on fire. I read the stories of the Bible like a private investigator looking for clues to disprove this whole Christianity thing. Except the more I studied and researched the more I discovered God had a plan! A plan of redemption that would set a sinful world free! It is a plan so perfect it would include making sinners like me look righteous in His sight. A plan so complete and Holy would free me from feeling flawed and foolish to being favored and forgiven. In short, it was a study that saved my life forever.

With this in mind, this entire book is based on a true story, my story with Him and His story for me. It is based on the truth from accounts given in scripture, showing us God's record of the divine-human encounter and how we fit into the boundless bliss of His grace. It is based on the true story of a sinner, like me, finding a Savior, like Jesus Christ, and His love that never changes.

I dedicate this book to my Lord and Savior, Jesus Christ.

This book is based on a true story.

Soli Christos, Soli Fidelis, Soli Deo Gloria.

Preface

People ask me, "How do we make Disciples at Antioch?" My ready response is now simple. We grow Disciples in Jesus Christ through Impact Ministry Groups. With this in mind, our Impact Ministry Groups are simply ministry models existing throughout the church and presented to empower us to fulfill the Great Commission and Great Commandment of our Lord Jesus Christ. Trust me when I say these groups are not just for fellowship. They serve, study, work, and grow disciples; those disciples make more disciples. Thus, the Great Commission and Great Commandment live for us at the church.

In this way, this devotional guide emerged. It grew out of a desire to press our church family closer together in what we sought to give the Lord as it pertains to Christian service. With this in mind, this small devotional guide will serve as our second Para source material, designed and developed by me to steer everyone at the church in the same direction.

This book is not a theological treatise on Christian doctrines and dogmas, though it contains some of both. It is simply a one-hundred-and-twenty-two-day study guide for the servant members of our congregation to read, hear, and hold fast to the magnificent stories of the Bible that carry us from the birth of Christ to the Cross of Christ. In short, He was born to die. After sharing this devotional study, I sincerely hope you will treasure the reality of knowing why.

Based On a True Story,

Dr. John R. Adolph, Pastor

Antioch Missionary Baptist Church

Acknowledgments

This work was born out of a deep desire to fulfill the Great Commission and the Great Commandment of our Lord Jesus Christ at Antioch Missionary Baptist Church, 3920 West Cardinal Drive, in the metropolis of Beaumont, Texas. When works like this come to fruition, it is never the result of the efforts of just one individual. It requires a collective composite of views, encounters, and skill sets to press it into production. This book is no different.

With this in mind, I must thank my personal Lord and Savior, Jesus Christ, for His death on the Cross at Calvary. I want to thank the Lord for His love for His bride, the church, and His patience with me as a Pastor. I'm forever indebted to Him as long as I live. May the works I have done please the Lord. May the grace that you have extended to me always speak for me.

To my wife of 27 years who has been by my side for everything, through my mother and father's passing, my failures and successes, through times of great joy and moments of testing and failure. Thank you so much, Lady Dorrie (Baby), for being steadfast, committed, prayerful, tolerant, loving, caring, faithful, earnest, loyal, and wonderful. May the Lord forever bless you is my sincerest prayer. Your growth in Christ as a disciple maker of women helped inspire this devotional work. Watching you teach them each Saturday morning made me want to share God's Will and Word with others even more.

To my wonderful children, Sumone and Jonathan, for supporting my work and ministerial sacrifice as a dad and pastor. Your growth in God as you matriculate at institutions of academic higher learning has made me so proud of you. I hope this book inspires you to one day pen your own work. Remember Philippians 4:13!

Thank you to my Executive Director of John R. Adolph Ministries, LLC, who also serves as the Chief of Administration of the church. Minister Brooklin Williams, thank you for connecting JRA Ministries with Advantage Publications and for your diligence, toil, time, and tenacity as it pertains to this book. I sincerely appreciate you.

To my Chief Executive Officers of Finance and Ministries, Felicia Young and Dr. Karen Davis, for encouraging me to write this devotional for our church family to use in our Impact Groups. And to Rev. Alfred Beverly II for designing the covers for nearly every book I've published. Your friendship means the world to me.

And to the full-time staff, part-time staff, and servant leaders of the Lord's Church at Antioch who partner with me in Kingdom building endeavors.

How to Use This Devotional Book

This small book is a one-hundred and twenty-two day journey designed for the members of Antioch Missionary Baptist Church of Beaumont, Texas. It is to share with one another as we seek to please the Lord through various modes of service and discipleship. Our Impact Ministry will use this guide each time they gather to grow in God's Word together, because we believe the Word of God revealed to us in scripture is BASED ON A TRUE STORY.

Instructions for Antioch Members

Listed below is the template every Impact Ministry Group should be using. The template is as follows:

IMPACT MINISTRY GROUPS

During Called Ministry Meetings
Add a (15) minute Bible Study
Take prayer requests and pray for one another
Intentionally care for the members of your ministry
Organize, develop, and implement times of faith, fun, and fellowship

For the members of your ministry

Foster Christian fellowships with a Minimum of at least 2 annually

Instructions for Non-Members

Let me begin by saying thank you for taking this journey! It is my prayer that it places a sincere desire to know, serve, and share the love of God with others like no other time in your life. With that said, plan a devotional time with the Lord. Please include a set place and time you plan to spend with God each day. Use this like you would a devotional journey.

Instructions for Everyone

The verses at the beginning of each entry are only referenced. With this in mind, please use your Bible and read the entire passage or verse. This will help you hear more of what the Lord says to you daily. After you read the scripture and the journal entry for the day, ask yourself the following devotional questions:

1. How does today's reading affect me?
2. What do I feel led to do after reading today's lesson?
3. What more could I do for the Lord based on what I just read?

Introduction

Hollywood, Tinseltown, Cinemark, Netflix, Hulu, and web-based television have reshaped the world we live in. I mean, think about it, the days of antennas, cable cords, satellite dishes, and TVs with knobs are a thing of the past. Television today is loaded with documentaries and docu-series filling the airways. People watch by the millions because they want to know the truth. We no longer want to know the story we see. We want to know the story behind the story that made the story we see get to the screen. This has led to movies that have soared at the box office and web-based TV based on a true story.

Think about it for a moment: Will Smith made us see the life of Mohammed Ali in a new light; Denzel Washington pushed Malcolm X to the forefront of our socio-cultural mindset. Chadwick Bozeman made James Brown dance again. Meryl Streep and Tom Hanks made the scandal of Watergate feel like we were sitting in the Nixon administration awaiting the secrets to hit the front page. Jamie Fox and Michael Jordan in the movie 'Just Mercy' made us feel the harsh reality of the story of Walter McMillian who was wrongfully convicted of a crime he did not commit. And the list goes on. The truth of the matter is this: We love films based on a true story.

When you open the pages of the Bible, the stories are like a movie on the silver screen. They are not myths, folklore, or legends. They are not just make-believe stories of the tooth fairy or Santa Claus. They are accounts BASED ON A TRUE STORY. The executive producer is God the Father, its chief editor is the Holy Ghost, and its fantastic lead actor is God incarnate, Jesus Christ!

This book is BASED ON A TRUE STORY. It is a one-hundred and twenty-one-day journey that will take you from the birth of Christ to the Cross of Christ in daily journals that should genuinely bless you—every thirty days, you can expect and anticipate something new. In the first thirty days, we will study true stories surrounding the birth of Jesus Christ. During our next thirty days, we will embrace the blessing of creation and the horror of sin, chaos, and confusion. Our last thirty days will look intently at the life of Jesus Christ, His death on the Cross, and His magnificent resurrection!

In short, we will journey from the crib to the Cross as we celebrate the redemptive plan of our loving God, with every account being A TRUE STORY!

Dr. John R. Adolph

Table of Contents

THE STORY OF THE BIRTH OF CHRIST

Day 1: Theo to the Rescue!

The Story of Theophilus, the Moneyman

It seemed good to me also, having had perfect understanding of all things from the very first, to write unto thee in order, most excellent Theophilus. (Luke 1:3)

Did you know the movie Ray, starring Jamie Foxx, cost over $40 million dollars to produce? It grossed over $124.7 million at the Box Office, making it a smash. What's the point here, you ask? If you are going to have an excellent production for others to hear and share a True Story someone must provide the economic resources for it to happen. When it comes to the story of Jesus Christ, as provided by Luke, the Physician, there is a story about a man whose name is only mentioned twice in the scriptures (Luke 1:3 & Acts 1:1). His name is Theophilus. His name means: *Friend of God or God's Good Friend.* It's believed when God got ready to produce the writings of Luke's Gospel; the financial resources needed for its production were graciously given by Theophilus. In this stead, we should shout Theo to the Rescue! We do not know how much money this wonderful man put on the table, however we do know the story of Jesus Christ is a box office smash. No figure in human history has been mentioned more than our Lord! No account rivals that of the True Story of Jesus Christ, and God blessed who took some of what He was blessed with so the world could hear the great news of Jesus Christ! Here's a solid devotional question for you to ponder: What do you do with the resources He has given you? Do you give so the Gospel can be heard around the world? If you don't, you should get started today!

Day 2: Don't Let the Gray Hair Fool You

The Story of Zacharias and Elizabeth

In the days of Herod, the King of Judaea, there was a certain priest named Zacharias, of the course of Abia, and his wife was the daughter of Aaron, and her name was Elisabeth. And they were both righteous before God, walking in all the commandments and ordinances of the Lord blamelessly. And they had no child because Elisabeth was barren, and they both were now well stricken in years. (Luke 1:5-7)

Some people dye it; even color it to avoid looking older. It was once seen as a symbol of wisdom; it came with great respect and honor attached. What is it you ask? Gray Hair - It suggests aging to the degree some would refer to people as a "Gray-headed fool"; others reference it as "The old gray dog ain't what he used to be". But such is not the case for Zacharias and Elizabeth. Here's a true story: Zacharias was an older man whom God chose to offer the sacrifices in the temple one day. When he got into the Holy Place, he saw the Angel Gabriel. Of course, Gabriel had an announcement to make. He told Zacharias he and his aged wife, Elizabeth, would be having a baby. In people's eyes, gray hair says, "You are out of commission and down for the count." Nevertheless, with the Lord, you are just right for the assignment if you can be found available and faithful. Here's the moral of the story: If you're available, God is able. It doesn't matter how old you may be. Zacharias and Elizabeth might have been gray, but don't let the gray hair fool you! Take a moment to ask the Lord this quick query: Lord, what's my assignment? Whisper this prayer to the Lord: I know you're able and I want you to know I'm available if you want to use me...in Jesus' name, Amen.

Day 3: Enter At Your Own Risk

The Story of Zacharias in the Temple

And it came to pass that while he executed the priest's office before God in the order of his course, According to the custom of the priest's office, his lot was to burn incense, when he went into the temple of the Lord. And the whole multitude of the people was praying without at the time of incense. (Luke 1:8-10)

"Enter at your own risk." It's the sign you see when you are about to walk into some stuff you might not walk out of. It could be better said like this, "I wouldn't go in there, if I were you." This is the feeling Zachariah felt when he walked into the temple that day, when he saw Gabriel. You see, when a priest went into the temple to offer up sacrifices, it could have been a deadly experience for him. In fact, they would tie a rope around his waist and attach a bell to the rope. They knew the priest was still alive if the cord was moving and the bell was ringing. Although, if the priest made a mistake and was judged by God on the spot, he would drop dead, and they could pull his lifeless body out without going in to get him. Zacharias goes into the temple. He's scared to death. Why? In the Holy presence of God, sin, error, human pride, and evil are not tolerated. Here's the moral of today's lesson: Don't play with God! He is Holy! He is righteous! He is flawless in every way. Don't play with God! He speaks, and men die. He speaks, and sick people who should have died, live on!

Day 4: Excuse Me; I Have an Announcement to Make

The Angel Gabriel Speaks Regarding Zacharias

And there appeared unto him an angel of the Lord standing on the right side of the altar of incense. And when Zacharias saw him, he was troubled, and fear fell upon him. But the angel said unto him, Fear not, Zacharias, for thy prayer is heard; and thy wife Elisabeth shall bear thee a son, and thou shalt call his name John. (Luke 1:11-13)

Unwanted, unexpected, and undesired announcements can get on your nerves. However, when the God of heaven and earth sends an angel to make one, you might want to shut up and pay close attention. When Zacharias enters the temple, he encounters an angel named Gabriel. The angel's countenance is bright. Zach is old, his heart is beating fast, and to make matters worse, Gabriel starts talking. He says, "Zach, don't be alarmed. I've got some good news for you, my friend; your prayers have been heard, and your wife Liz will have a baby. Don't call him Junior, call him John!" Here's what's not mentioned in this story; great for a moment of devotion. Zacharias prayed for a son all of his life. God does not bless him with one until he is an old man. Here's the shout of the day: God is always good on His promises. You may be delayed, but you are never denied. You might have to wait, but your wait will always be worth it. You may even feel like God has forgotten about you. Nevertheless, God's memory is so good; He never has to remember anything, because He cannot ignore it.

Day 5: I See Him In The Future; and He Looks Good

Zacharias' Prophecy about John

And thou shalt have joy and gladness; and many shall rejoice at his birth. For he shall be great in the sight of the Lord, and shall drink neither wine nor strong drink; and he shall be filled with the Holy Ghost. .And he shall go before him in the spirit and power of Elias, to turn the hearts of the fathers to the children, and the disobedient to the wisdom of the just; to make ready a people prepared for the Lord. (Luke 1:14-17)

How would you rejoice if God sent you a prophecy that he favored your children? What would you do, if the Lord sent the prophecy by an angel? What if the angel declared your son would not be an ordinary man, but an extraordinary man filled with the presence of God, reminding the world of the great Prophet Elijah? This took place for Zacharias in the temple that day he went in. Gabriel unloaded on him! By now, Zacharias is starting to think he's losing his mind. Angels are talking, the rope around his waist ain't moving, the bell tied to his waist isn't ringing, and the folks outside waiting on him to come out are starting to think he's dead. Yet nothing could be further from the truth. Not only is he alive, he is receiving news God is about to bless his son. Here's the shout; it is the son he does not have yet. Sometimes in life, you have to trust God at His Word and move on. Just because you can't see it does not mean you will not have it in the future. If you could see what the Lord has planned not just for your children but for you, it would cause you to rejoice in His name, no matter what your current conditions look like. You should practice right quick and tell the Lord, "Thank you!" Greater is on the way!

Day 6: Hush! I'll Let You Know When You Can Talk

Zacharias Can't Say A Word

And, behold, thou shalt be dumb, and not able to speak, until the day that these things shall be performed, because thou believest not my words, which shall be fulfilled in their season. (Luke 1:20)

There are times in life when doubt creeps in under the radar like a Black Hawk helicopter, causing believers to stumble. Has it ever happened to you? If you can say yes, then you understand the story of Zacharias in the temple. You see, he's just been told by an angel he and his aged wife Elizabeth are going to be having a son. There are significant problems with this announcement. First, the couple is way too old to have kids. Second, they're supposed to call his name John because he will be the forerunner for Jesus Christ. Lastly, when Zacharias has questions, Gabriel, the angel, says, "Hush, I'll let you know when you can talk since you didn't believe my announcement." So when Zacharias walked out of the temple that day, he was using his hands to talk; he could not say a word for nine months! Here's our point of devotional celebration: Zacharias loved the Lord so much that he would use his hands if he couldn't talk. And if he couldn't have used his hands, he would have just rocked from side to side. When God blesses you, live in the moment; take everything for what it is!

Day 7: You'll Never Guess Who's Pregnant

Elizabeth Conceives

And after those days his wife Elisabeth conceived, and hid herself five months, saying, Thus hath the Lord dealt with me in the days wherein he looked on me, to take away my reproach among men. (Luke 1:24-25)

It's news that sounds like hot gossip in a beauty shop, right? It even gives the feeling of a rerun from a heavily viewed episode of Jerry Springer. Now, here's what's crazy: It is a true story straight from the pages of the Bible. Elisabeth gets pregnant. Okay, let's tell the whole story. Zach, her hubby, comes home from the temple, and he's been endowed with a burst of energy and feeling himself. He hugs his wife, kisses her forehead and says "I feel like a young man, Liz" (JRA Version)! And from that moment came passion, intimacy, and a pregnancy. Elisabeth was so shocked she kept the news of her pregnancy a secret for five months. Here's the blessing of today's true story: God did just what He said! The gift of grace bestowed upon every believer is that the Lord is always faithful….always!

Day 8: Highly Favored and Blessed

The Angel Gabriel Visits Mary in Nazareth

And the angel came in unto her, and said, Hail, thou that art highly favored, the Lord is with thee, blessed art thou among women. And when she saw him, she was troubled at his saying and cast in her mind what manner of salutation this should be. (Luke 1:28-29)

The presence of God in any story makes an ordinary narrative extraordinary. If you add Jesus to a wedding, water becomes wine. If you add God to the celebration of Pentecost, Peter becomes a preacher, and three-thousand people get saved. If you add the Lord to a kid's snack with only two fish and five small crackers, it can become a seafood buffet for five-thousand with leftovers. And, if you add the presence of Christ to the life of a teenage virgin, she can conceive and have a baby that could save the world from sin. My friend, today's true story brings us to the socioeconomically challenged city of Nazareth, where Mary has discovered three things. She now knows angels can talk. She knows virgins can get pregnant, and she knows something good can come from the hood. Here's our devotional highpoint of the day: God favors what He wants to favor and blesses what He wants to bless! In His sovereign majesty, it's not where you are from that causes Him to favor and bless you. It's about His life-changing plans for your life that does. Live in God's favor and walk in His blessing every day of your life.

Day 9: The Gender Reveal

Gabriel Tells Mary She's Going To Have a Son

And the angel said unto her, "Fear not, Mary, for thou hast found favor with God. And, behold, thou shalt conceive in thy womb, and bring forth a son, and shalt call his name Jesus. (Luke 1:30-31)

Gender reveal parties are a booming business, as it relates to modern-day family matters. People cut cakes, burst balloons, even have helicopters drop colored powder on outdoor parties, to name a few. However, no gender reveal has ever been as extravagant as the one in our story today. An angel robed in the glorious white light of heaven stops by the tough part of the region in a city called Nazareth to tell a teenager she will be the mother of a baby boy! Of course, virgins don't have babies, so it makes this story that much more miraculous, and the gender reveal will probably never be duplicated ever again. Here's a great devotional query to ponder, as you journey through your day. Has God ever revealed Himself to you in a unique way? What took place? How did He do it? Cherish moments when the Lord makes Himself real to you and tell others the truth of your story every time you get a chance.

Day 10: What Are You Gonna Name Him

His Name Will Be Above Every Name

And the angel said unto her, Fear not, Mary, for thou hast found favor with God. And, behold, thou shalt conceive in thy womb, and bring forth a son, and shalt call his name Jesus. (Luke 1:30-31)

People call their children just about anything these days. Such was not the case just a few years ago. Names had specific meanings and significance. If you wanted to honor someone in a great and noble way, you would bear a child, and give the child the name of the person you sought to pay honor and respect to. However, such would not be the case when naming Mary's baby. In our true story today, Gabriel instructs Mary not to name her son after her soon-to-be husband, Joseph. She's warned not to name her son after her biological father, Joachim. Do not name him any other name. Mary is told to name her son Jesus! Yeshua (Joshua in Hebrew). It means great deliverer or savior. His name means the one who saves. Mary would later discover wise men would seek her son for worship, and His name would be honored on earth, feared in hell, and worshipped in heaven, forever. Jesus is His name! Here's a devotional question for you to ponder. What does His name mean to you? What does His name say to you? Why do you think His name is so important? Always remember there is salvation in His name, healing in His name, life in His name, blessing in His name, joy in His name, and power in His name! His name is above every name!

Day 11: Hold Up, I've got a Question

Mary Wants To Know How Is This Going to Happen

Then said Mary unto the angel, "How shall this be, seeing I know not a man?" (Luke 1:34)

Sometimes, we have questions in life only God can answer. Then we raise our hand like a child in grade school sitting in the back of class; clear our throat, and say, "Hold Up, I've Got a Question?" If it hasn't happened to you yet, just keep on living. It happened to Mary, the mother of Jesus, as a teenager. Gabriel shows up with one of his famous announcements, telling her she will be having a baby. Then, she cleared her throat, raised her hand, and said, "I've got a question: How is that supposed to happen when I have not been with any guy intimately?" This question is good old common sense, right? But remember: Whenever you walk with God, our common sense leads to nonsense because He has the power no one else has! The great news is God isn't bothered by our questions. He has the power, ability, and authority to do whatever He wants to do, when He wants to. Here's a very real devotional question for you to ponder: What queries do you have for God that cause you to raise your hand and say, "Hold Up, I've Got a Question?" Keep this in mind: God doesn't have to answer. But if He does, remember, you can trust Him because He has proven Himself trustworthy.

Day 12: God's Got It Covered

How God Is Going To Do It Is Not Your Concern

And the angel answered and said unto her, "The Holy Ghost shall come upon thee, and the power of the Highest shall overshadow thee. Therefore also that Holy thing, which shall be born of thee shall be called the Son of God. (Luke 1:35)

Frederica Sanders was facing foreclosure, a sudden cutback at her job, and serious issues with anxiety and stress. Her eight-year-old grandson saw her at the kitchen table and said, "Me-Maw, I can tell you are stressing over something. Don't worry, God's got it covered!" Keep this in mind, *how* God is going to do what He does is not your concern. Mary wants to know how this promised pregnancy is going to take place when she is still a virgin. Gabriel lets her know the Holy Ghost would rest on her and the presence of the Lord shall cover her. He then affirms what is happening in her life is God's business, and He has everything covered. I don't know exactly what obstacles, issues, or problems you might face, as you share this moment of personal devotion. It could be a diagnosis that looks bleak or a bankruptcy, which is just bad. It could be a marital woe causing you to lose sleep or a wayward child you cannot get settled. Whatever the case or cause, the gracious news of the day is God's got it covered! The same God who causes a virgin to have the promised Messiah for every sinner on earth is the same Lord who cares for our daily needs and concerns. Think about your most significant problem. Now whisper this prayer: "God's got it covered. In Jesus' name…Amen!"

Day 13: You're Not the Only One

Your Story Is Not an Isolated Incident

And, behold, thy cousin Elisabeth, she hath also conceived a son in her old age, and this is the sixth month with her, who was called barren. (Luke 1:36)

The blessing of a true story is it gives an accurate report of what took place in the lives of someone else. A true story is a testimony of the test of another that can bear witness to what was done in their lives, as proof God can do it in your life should He choose to. Gabriel lets Mary know, "You're not the only one!" Mary is informed her cousin Elizabeth, who is old, is now pregnant. Here's the shout: Elizabeth is not too old, and Mary is not too young. Elizabeth was not out of commission, and Mary, though never having a marital moment of consummation, was still just right for God's plan. What a story! God has chosen two women faced with the physiological impossibilities of having a child, and His favor removes all boundaries, limits, and barriers that could block the blessed plan of the creator to save a dying world from sin. You see, here's the root of this story: You're not the only one God has healed. You're not the only one who has gone from expecting God to fulfill a promise to live the promise God sought faithfully to fulfill. You are not the only one the Lord has chosen to do something amazing through and for. Knowing there are others should cause you to thank Him for choosing to bless you the way He has.

Day 14: Nothing Shall Be Impossible

The Story of Mary and Elizabeth

For with God nothing shall be impossible. (Luke 1:37)

It can be one of the most insulting terms ever used and one of the most painful places to dwell. To be told you are worth nothing, or to tell a hungry family you have nothing to offer, to be in a place economically where you have nothing. In short, nothing can be a harsher. But the moment you add the person of God to the equation, the word nothing takes on a different vibe. For with God, I need nothing. By the grace of God, my nothing added to His everything gives me something to live for every day. And, when you look at the true story of the character of God and how He exists beyond the boundaries of spatial limits, the celebration of the people of faith is there is nothing our God cannot do. Mary and Elizabeth's cause brings us to one conclusion. If God can take an older woman who is beyond her years of childbearing and cause her to have a child, and if God can take a virgin and cause her to have a baby, there is nothing our God cannot do. It's why verses like the one mentioned before should remain in your heart forever. It is again penned for your study. May it rest, rule, and remain with you forever, for nothing shall be impossible with God.

Day 15: I Choose To Believe

Mary's Response to God's Promise

And Mary said, Behold the handmaid of the Lord; be it unto me according to thy word. And the angel departed from her. (Luke 1:38)

There are times belief makes no sense at all. Yet, by faith, we choose to believe it. When Gabriel tells Mary she will have a baby, her response is shocking. She said, "Be it unto me according to thy word." In short, "I choose to believe." Mary's reply is what pushes the entire Christian faith. It is the root of salvation and the fruit of our hope. Whatever is it you ask? She believes! It is the moment of volitional approval based not on feelings or facts, but faith in what the Lord has promised. She chooses to believe! It is a matter of personal discretion used to promote God's miraculous agenda in her life. Mary says, "If God said it that settles it because I believe it!" That's Mary's true story. What is yours? Do you choose God at what He has said, or does doubt ever choke your belief to death? Have you ever reached the place in your walk with Jesus Christ where your beliefs affect your behavior? Have you arrived at the threshold of faith where what you believe in God causes you to worry less and trust much more? Remember this: When you choose to believe, the Lord will soon bless you in extraordinary life-changing ways.

Day 16: The Baby Has It Right

John's Response to the Presence of Jesus

And it came to pass, that, when Elisabeth heard the salutation of Mary, the babe leaped in her womb; and Elisabeth was filled with the Holy Ghost. (Luke 1:41)

So, here's how the story goes. When Mary leaves Gabriel, she decides to head to the hill country to visit her older cousin, Elizabeth, who is about six-months pregnant with John, the Baptist. When Mary gets to the house and says hello to Elizabeth, her baby gets happy in her belly and starts shouting for joy! In other words, a six-month-old fetus in his mother's womb rejoices at the presence of Jesus, who is three months old in His mother's womb. John, the six-month-old baby in Elizabeth's womb has it right. You must ask yourself the intelligent question: Why is John, at only six-months-old, rejoicing and jumping around in his mother's belly? Is it because Jesus has performed a miracle? Is John leaping for joy because Jesus resurrected someone from the dead? Why is a six-month-old unborn baby shouting in His mother's womb when he gets near Jesus, who is only three months old? Here's the honest answer: John is rejoicing because he is in the presence of His King! Now, if a six-month-old unborn fetus can rejoice in the presence of the Lord, what should your response while in His presence? Rejoice now, while you have a chance, because practice makes perfect.

Day 17: I've Just Got to Praise Him

The Story of Mary's Worship in Judea

And Mary said, "My soul doth magnify the Lord, and my spirit hath rejoiced in God my Savior." (Luke 1:46-47)

Praise is an expression of gratitude given to a recipient counted worthy of such honor by those who believe it necessary. Who is the recipient of your praise? Who in your life is considered honorable in receiving it? Here's a true story. Before Mary had her baby, and while Elizabeth was still pregnant, Mary honored the Lord with her praise, because she found Him to be her worthy recipient. Mary realizes the Lord decided to bless her when He could have chosen anyone. She had come to grips with the fact that what God is doing through her is not just for her but for generations yet to come. She understands God has chosen one of the least to impact those considered great! In this, God has chosen her to be the mother of God, and He deserves all praise and glory for what He has done.

Day 18: The Blessing of Good Company

The Story of Mary with Elizabeth at the Birth of John

And Mary abode with her about three months, and returned to her own house.....And her neighbours and her cousins heard how the Lord had shewed great mercy upon her; and they rejoiced with her. (Luke 1:56-58)

If bad company corrupts good manners, it stands to reason that good company constructs great camaraderie. Just think about it for a moment. Time spent with negative people can make even the most positive people negative. However, if you can spend quality time with good people, you are blessed by the Lord with some good company. Here's the true story for the day: when Mary visited Elizabeth in the Hill Country, she stayed for about three months. And when she departed, Elizabeth gave birth to John the Baptist and was surrounded by neighbors, cousins, and family. Here's the question of the day: how do you know when good company is good? The answer is simple. Good company grieves when you are hurt, smiles when you are happy, and celebrates when God blesses you as if He had just blessed them. Take a moment and survey those people who make up your concentric circle of contacts, and ask yourself this question: Are you blessed with good company? If so, thank God for them; if not, find new friends in the faith.

Day 19: I Told You It Was Going To Happen

The Birth of Jesus was foretold

Now all this was done that it might be fulfilled, which was spoken of the Lord by the prophet. Saying, behold, a virgin shall be with child, and shall bring forth a son, and they shall call his name Emmanuel, which being interpreted is, God with us. (Matthew 1:21)

What makes the story of the birth of Jesus so unique is it was foretold years before it actually happened. In the prophetic annals of the writings of Isaiah, we have the words foretold concerning the birth of our Lord. In this regard, prophecy is best defined as history written in advance. It is tomorrow's news today. Like knowing who the championship winner will be before the series starts or the game is even played. Isaiah says, "I'm telling you right now, a virgin is going to have a baby, and His name will be called Emmanuel." This one name is so powerful. It suggests God became one of us. It is the realization of the incarnation. God, who is a spirit, will put on an earth suit of flesh. Now, this story shouts that to redeem a thing; you must become the thing you seek to redeem. The celebration of this passage is Isaiah said it would happen, and it did! The prophet said it would take place, and it came to pass without fail. It was as if Matthew and Isaiah got together somehow, and the Holy Spirit stamped this story as true. The great news of the day is this story gives Isaiah the bragging rights because he could say "I told you it was going to happen!

Day 20: My Dream Feels like A Nightmare

Joseph's Response to Mary's Being Pregnant

Then Joseph her husband, being a just man, and not willing to make her a public example, was minded to put her away privily....behold, the angel of the Lord appeared unto him in a dream, saying....that which is conceived in her is of the Holy Ghost. (Matthew 1:19-20)

We always hear Mary's story during the Christmas season and rightfully so. However, we rarely hear the story of Joseph, her husband. Can you imagine your spouse telling you she's pregnant before the honeymoon? Can you imagine the thoughts running through his mind? Let's borrow from reality TV for just a moment, please! He thought the guy in the market always wanted to help her with her groceries, right? Or even the handsome guy with the rich dad always speaks to her. Joseph's mind is going a thousand miles a minute. Except, here's what Joseph did that helped his dream not feel like a nightmare. He held in what he pondered; he held up under pressure, and he held onto the promise the Lord made him. The great news of this story is Joseph was not superhuman. He had feelings, questions, doubts, and concerns just like anyone else, if they found themselves in a similar predicament. And, the same God who stopped his dream from becoming a nightmare will do the same thing for you!

Day 21: In Those Days

The World Jesus Was Born Into

And it came to pass in those days, that there went out a decree from Caesar Augustus that all the world should be taxed. (Luke 2:1-2)

Here's something radically true about the story of Jesus Christ. The world He was born into was already old. As Christians, we often see the birth of Jesus as the start of time itself. However, this needs to be more accurate. It is, nevertheless, the start of a new era in which God would show us His grace in a whole new dimension. A grace so amazing God Himself would die like a criminal on the Cross for sinners like us. Yet, here's the truth of the matter: The world was already old. Governments had risen and fallen; kingdoms came and went, others faded away. Rulers had risen, and history records that rulers had found their demise. But, when the time was perfect God let Mary and Joseph make their way to the city of Bethlehem for the birth of our Savior, Jesus Christ. Here's the devotional blessing from today's true story: God uses time to promote His agenda because He is not bound by it. In short, God never grows old; He never runs out of time. The phrase "in those days" in the Bible, can be better translated as, "according to God's plan when time was just right." When Jesus was born, Rome ruled the world. Today, our world is guided by governments and powers on every continent. Still, our God always reigns no matter what empires have risen and fallen!

Day 22: Taxes, Travel, and Travail

Joseph and Mary make their way to Bethlehem

And all went to be taxed; everyone into his own city. (Luke 2:3)

In America, our Census takes place so we can count the people claiming this country as their home. Taxes are what we pay, if we are going to work and earn a living. In the days of Jesus, the Roman government had a way of pretty much doing the same thing. People returned to their homes to be counted and to pay taxes to the government. So here's the story: Mary and Joseph must travel from Nazareth to Bethlehem for the government's census and tax payments. It was about a ninety-mile journey lasting at least four days, moving on the back of a donkey at a speed of about two to five miles an hour. Can you imagine? To add insult to injury, Mary is due any moment, now. Her feet are swollen, her contractions are intensifying, and the bumps throughout the terrain are merciless. The sun is scorching, the heat is damaging, no position is comfortable, and the trip never ends. All of this travel and travail to pay taxes? Absolutely not! It is to make sure the one who would declare Himself to be the bread of life is located in the house of bread, Bethlehem, at just the right time! Here's a great question to ponder: Has God ever done something in your life? Something you didn't understand at the time, but through the lenses of hindsight made you say it had to happen this way? What was it? Take a moment to thank God for it!

Day 23: The House of Bread

Mary and Joseph in Bethlehem

And Joseph also went up from Galilee, out of the city of Nazareth, into Judaea, unto the city of David, which is called Bethlehem; (because he was of the house and lineage of David) (Luke 2:4)

The Hebrew term Bethlehem is a beautiful word composite of two terms. Beth in Hebrew means "house". Lehem translates "of bread." When you combine these two terms, Bethlehem means *House of Bread*. The true story behind the name of this city - it was the place where both Jews and Gentiles came together. Ruth married Boaz in Bethlehem. Most importantly, it is the birthplace of our Jewish King, who would openly declare "I am the bread of life, he that comes to me will never hunger and he that believes shall never thirst" (John 6:35, KJV). Bethlehem is where the world meets its Savior who saves sinners from sin. It is the place where God shows the rest of the world the grace needed for humankind, especially those who are not our kind. Here's the shout for the day: God could have had His birth in any city in the known world. He could have been born in Egypt, Babylon, or even Rome. Instead, He uses the tiny town of Bethlehem because Jesus is the bread of life for every nation!

Day 24: She's Heavy Pregnant

Mary Is Due Any Moment Now

To be taxed with Mary his espoused wife, being great with child. And so it was, that, while they were there, the days were accomplished that she should be delivered. (Luke 2:5-6)

Have you ever heard the phrase "heavy pregnant"? It's typically used to reference a woman who is not just with a child; the child is so close to making its entry; her water could break at any moment. It suggests the fetus is sitting on her pelvis bone. It means there will be some action in the near future. Here's the story for today's devotional: When Mary and Joseph arrived at Bethlehem, it was all Mary could stand. She is pregnant and about to deliver the child who will be born, Christ, King, and Messiah! It is like a promise about to come to pass. It is like the gift on Christmas day about to be torn open. It is like the check you have been waiting for to come in the mail and you just discovered UPS is knocking at your door with the package in hand. In this story, Jesus is almost here. In many cases, celebrations like this should start early. If you celebrate your birthday all month long, you should be shouting right now because Mary is about to have her baby.

Day 25: She Just Had the Baby

Jesus our Savior is Born

And she brought forth her firstborn son, and wrapped him in swaddling clothes, and laid him in a manger; because there was no room for them in the inn. (Luke 2:7)

The annals of Roman history give credence and credibility to the fact Jesus was born. Mary, Joseph, Simeon, and Anna the Prophetess testify Jesus was born. A well-rounded group of Magi, which may have numbered as many as three hundred men, followed a star coming from the east, confirm the fact Jesus was born. Members of the caravan traveling from Nazareth to Bethlehem will tell you Jesus was born. The shepherds keeping their flocks in the field who saw heaven roll back like a scroll with angels rejoicing and singing will tell you Jesus was born. If we were to interview the evil conscientious likes of King Herod who really wanted Jesus dead can say to you Jesus was born! And those of you who have chosen to believe by faith can personally attest there is no day on earth like today! Today is the greatest day, which time on earth has ever seen! The word has become flesh; divinity has become humanity; the eternal, boundless grace of glory is now wearing a body made of flesh. God has become one of us to save us from sin, Satan, and self. Oh praise His name! Merry Christmas, and to God be the glory!

Day 26: When the Stars Tell the Story

The Wise Men Seek Jesus

Now when Jesus was born in Bethlehem of Judaea in the days of Herod the King, behold, there came wise men from the east to Jerusalem, saying, Where is he that is born King of the Jews? For we have seen his star in the east, and are come to worship him. (Matthew 2:1-2)

For centuries, galaxy gazers have used the stars to provide direction, instruction, and wisdom. Men and women in the United States Navy believe in the constellation of stars called the Little Dipper and the Big Dipper. When Harriet Tubman led enslaved people to freedom from the heated racism of the South to the liberated boundaries of the North, they were blessed with the guidance of the North Star. When people are considering long-term relational constructs, they often look to their horoscope for signs of relational compatibility. Here's a true story of galaxy-gazers and star-watchers given in the scriptures. A collage of wise men from the east, numbering as many as three hundred men possibly from the region of Arabia, had been galaxy gazing for centuries. They were waiting for the arrival of the promised Son of God, and when they spotted a specific star in the East, they followed it in pursuit of the one they would call King. Have you ever ask yourself the question, "What was it that made the wise men so wise?" The only answer that arises from a question like this is to understand what made them wise is seeking Christ, who is the source of all wisdom. It may be better put like this: Wise men still seek Him!

Day 27: Problems at the Home Front

Herod is confronted by the Wise Men Looking for the King

When Herod the King heard these things, he was troubled, and all Jerusalem with him. Then Herod, called the wise men, inquired of them diligently what time the star appeared. And he sent them to Bethlehem, and said, "Go and search diligently for the young child; and when ye have found him, bring me word again, that I may come and worship him also." (Matthew 2:3-8)

So here's the true story. Herod is a king, however, the Wise Men show up looking for the one who was born the King. Can you feel the tension? Herod is a king, but Jesus is the King! When Herod is confronted by a group of men looking for the King he is troubled. Why is he worried? Here's the easy answer: There is only room for one King! The Wise Men are not looking for him; they are looking for Jesus! Here's a great question to think about: Do you serve a king or the King? If you are wise, you will serve the Lord Jesus Christ, for He alone is King of kings and Lord of lords!

Day 28: The Night Heaven Got Happen

Shepherds see Angels Rejoicing in Heaven

And suddenly there was with the angel a multitude of the heavenly host praising God, and saying, glory to God in the highest, and on earth peace, goodwill toward men. (St. Luke 2:13-14)

Imagine you are working the nightshift. You settle in for the evening, the dark of night falls upon you and your co-workers. As time passes, the night darkens, the silence thickens. Suddenly, you see a bright light shining from heaven. The sky rolls back like a scroll, you see angelic beings shouting and rejoicing like crazy. Your first reaction is to run; except you realize there is nowhere to go. So you decide to gaze up, listen up, and make your focus the upward way of eternal glory. Then you hear an angel, he says, "Don't panic! There's nothing to be afraid of; we are shouting because a baby is being born in Bethlehem. He is God's gift to a dying world! He is heaven wrapped in a body!" And while you are looking up, you see a choir shouting and singing "On earth peace, goodwill toward men!" Then, you realize the gulf once separating heaven and earth has been connected. A bridge has been constructed, and the toll has been paid! Here's a question for you to consider: If heaven can rejoice, why can't you? Praise the name of Jesus Christ! For He alone is worthy to be praised!

Day 29: GPS Is Back On and Popping

The Star Reappears and the Wise Men Worship

When they saw the star, they rejoiced with exceeding great joy. And when they were come into the house, they saw the young child with Mary his mother, and fell down, and worshipped him. And when they had opened their treasures, they presented unto him gifts; gold, and frankincense and myrrh. (Matthew 2:10-11)

It can be very frustrating. You load the address into your GPS. You know you are completely lost without it. You are one of those people who are geographically challenged. You start your journey, your GPS says, "Signal lost." It can leave you feeling empty and vain. Have you ever been there? If you have, you know what the Wise Men felt while following the star. You see, while following the star it disappeared. We are still determining exactly what happened to it. Perhaps, the night became cloudy, and the clouds consumed it. The night took on different cosmological constructs and hid it. Whatever the case, we do not know precisely why it was lost from sight. But here's the shout: It reappeared! The Wise Men found Jesus, and they worshipped Him! Here's a query to ponder: What blocks you from sincere worship? Here's the moral of today's lesson: When it comes to worshipping your King, let nothing get in your way.....NOTHING!

Day 30: The Right Place at the Right Time

The Story of Simeon and Anna in the Temple

And, behold, there was a man in Jerusalem named Simeon; the same man was just and devout...and there was one Anna, a prophetess, the daughter of Phanuel... (St. Luke 2:25 & 2:36)

Being in the right place at the right time can bless you like crazy! During Hurricane Harvey relief efforts in Southeast Texas, blessings fell on those who were in the right place at the right time. For example, you could have received gas cards for free gas, HEB cards for free water and groceries, even disaster relief assistance to help you rebuild your damaged home. It did not always happen for everyone, yet it did happen for those who were in the right place at the right time. So it was for both Simeon and Anna. They were both found in the temple when Jesus was born and were blessed in some amazing ways. Simeon declared he "...Would not see death until he had seen the Lord's Christ" (Luke 2:25). Anna was a Prophetess who dedicated her life to fasting and prayer in the temple until she could see the Christ child. When she saw Him, she thanked the Lord for His redemption being ever-present. You see, both Simeon and Anna were in the right place at the right time. Here's a question: If you could see Jesus face to face, what would you say to Him? What would be your response? Here's the good news: Practice makes perfect! One of these days, you will see Him, and on that day, you want to hear Him say, "Servant, well done!"

Day 31: Don't Go Back the Same You Came

The Wise Men Go Home A New Way

And being warned of God in a dream….they departed into their home country another way. (Matthew 2:12)

Perfection is one thing; however, redemptive change is another. The difference between these two is huge. Perfection is fleeting and seldom comes. But redemption happens the moment you encounter Jesus Christ! You can be sure your life will never be the same at that moment. Jesus Christ is not just a soul saver; He's a life changer! The true story of this passage is after the Wise Men find Jesus; they worship Him because He is the only one on earth worthy of their worship. The Wise Men bring Jesus gold fit for a King, frankincense made for a prophet; and myrrh for a priest who looks to do His job as an intercessor well. When these wonderful men prepare to leave the presence of the Lord, they are warned by God in a dream not to return home the same way they came. Going home is a good thing; just go home with some degree of change. Actually, no one should worship the Lord and leave His presence the same way. Something in your life should be better, changed, altered, rearranged, or transformed. His presence has that effect on all of us! Be honest and ponder this thought: In what ways have you encountered the Lord and gone home a different way?

THE STORY OF CREATION

Dr. John R. Adolph

Day 32: When God Goes In

In the beginning, God created the heavens and the earth. (Genesis 1:1)

It is a common phrase heard whenever people show off some of their true potential. Then, you hear people say, "They went in." It happens when a cook in the kitchen knows their expertise well and comes out with a masterpiece, a meal that's finger-licking good. You will often hear people say, "They went in." When a running back runs hard the entire game and ends the contest victorious with 100 yards rushing and 20 yards receiving, it is easy for sportscasters to say, "They went in!" Here's a great devotional question for you to ponder as we begin our devotional time in the study of God in creation: Has God ever gone in? Consider this: God spoke, and worlds were formed; He declared and decreed it, and rivers and mountains were birthed. He demanded it, and oceans and seas had places to live! Our God in creation did not only create the earth, but the shout for us is: He created every galaxy known to humankind, and those yet to be discovered. He put moons around Pluto and rings around Saturn. He gave Mars its red dirt, the Sun its shine, the Moon its glow, and the Earth's inhabitants the right to live! Hear this: Our God is an awesome God. When He created the heavens and the earth, it was His way of saying let it be known that "I went in!"

Day 33: When Hell Breaks Loose

And the earth was without form, and void; and darkness was upon the face of the deep. (Genesis 1:2a)

Hell can happen anywhere the forces of darkness and evil spirits have their way. It is what happened in Genesis 1:2a. You will notice in Chapter 1, God created the heavens and the earth. In verse two of the same chapter, you will see the planet is void and without form; darkness is upon the face of the deep. God has never created anything dark, void, or without purpose. We believe something catastrophic happened to the Earth in Genesis Chapter one, Verse two. Here is what we believe took place. Lucifer and two-thirds of the Angelic hosts were evicted from heaven, and the earth became their new domain place. The great news of this story is the difference between a domain and having dominion. The shout of the day is: Our God still has dominion. The enemy has the earth as his domain. What proof do we have of such taking place? The evidence in the passage lets us know the earth had a moment when it was dark and void. Doesn't this sound like the work of the enemy? God has never made anything dark and void. The good news is hell may break loose, but heaven will win in the end! As you study this devotional series, remember you will win because God is on your side. On a personal note, have you ever felt like you were in a dark place? Have you ever felt like your life had no purpose? Nothing could be further from the truth! Just like hell broke loose on the earth, it could also break loose in our lives. But just like hell can break loose, so can heaven. The prayer for today in your life is for heaven to rule, reign, and have regency all day long!

Day 34: When Spirit Moves

And the Spirit of God moved upon the face of the waters. (Genesis 1:2b)

As Christians, we believe in the Trinity. This concept suggests God is one in essence yet three personalities. It means that God, for us, is a Father who adopted us into his royal family. It means we have a Son who is God in the flesh, whose name is Jesus Christ. It also means we have a Spirit called the Holy Ghost. Each of these personalities makes God who He is. When you read Genesis 1:2, you find the Spirit of God is present. And not only is He present, He is large and in charge! The Spirit shows up and recreates a masterpiece. Sadly, the Spirit moved. It should be known, whenever the Spirit of God moves, God Himself is at work! And when God works, nothing remains the same. In this passage, God is about to take an earth that is void without form and give it a brand new life. God is about to take what looks like a waste and cause it to become the place we now call home. God, by way of the Spirit, is about to transform the entire planet into a place for humans to live. Who else but God could take a complete waste and make it worthwhile? Before you answer, ask yourself this question: Has God ever taken my waste and sin and graced me with something much greater? Have you ever seen God move in your life in such a way it transformed everything around you? Here is the shout for today: To meet God in the person of his Spirit is to meet God and never be the same! It only happens when the Spirit moves!

Day 35: Turn the Lights On

And God said, Let there be light: and there was light. (Genesis 1:3)

It is a common saying heard when people walk into a dark abode. It is expected to hear the exact phrase when a child is about to be left in a room without their parents to sleep throughout the night. Have you ever heard of it before? Have you heard what you ask? The phrase is, "Turn the lights on!". If you have never heard that phrase before, let me invite you into a study of Genesis 1:3. In this passage, God is about to take the black of night and make it look like the brightness of the day! God is about to take what appears a hopeless dark moment and cause it to become a hopeful day of light and divine expectation. When you study the passage listed above, it should cause you to feel a sense of hope in any situation. If God can take the pitch-black darkness of outer space, and cause it to have light, you know He can handle any darkness you will ever face! If you ask the question: How did God do it? The answer would be simply this: He spoke it into existence! Friends, God, operated by faith, spoke to nothing so something could exist. God put faith on display as he took what would have been eternal darkness and gave us everlasting light! Ponder this interrogative for a moment: How dark would your life be if God were not in it? What light would you have, if you didn't have God walking with you every day? Here's the shout of the day, and do not forget it. As long as the Lord is the light of your day, you will never walk in darkness! We know this to be true because our God says to the darkness, "Let there be light!"

Day 36: Night and Day |The First Day

And God called the light day, and the darkness he called night. And the evening and the morning were the first day. (Genesis 1:5)

Ray Charles Robinson was one of the greatest artists of our time. Ray Charles had numerous hits that stayed on the charts in the number one spot for months at a time. "Hit the Road Jack" was just one of them. People of every race, creed and color, all around America, danced when they heard his music. One song in particular was one of his most popular hits. It was entitled "Night and Day"! Even though this passage has nothing to do with the music of Ray Charles, its subject matter begs to differ. You see, in this passage, God shows Ray Charles what night and day are both composed of. When you read the passage listed above, it is a must God receives the credit, the glory, and the gratitude for showing all of humanity night and day. On every continent, we have night and day. In every culture, we are exposed to night and day. In everyplace under the sun, we must come to grips with night and day. Ray may have put music to it, but God has the supreme rule over it. While Ray may have had people dancing to its beat, God had the universe moving to His rhythm. The sun rises, sets, and the moon reflects the sun and glows. What a mighty God, we serve! If we could look at night and day metaphorically, what season of life are you in right now? The night, where things are dark? Or the day when things have light? Here's the great news: It does not matter whether life is dark or you are walking in the light. God controls both night and day! Oh, praise His name!

Day 37: The Sky's the Limit|The Second Day

And God said, "Let there be a firmament in the midst of the waters and let it divide the waters from the waters." And the evening and the morning were the second day. (Genesis 1:6-8)

There was a story of a teacher in an elementary school helping students with their spelling tests. One student, who had an excellent test, made a score of one-hundred percent. What a perfect test score in hand! The zealous student asked the teacher what more they could do. The teacher replied, "The sky is the limit!" When you hear comments like "the sky's the limit," it should press you to know something important. There have been moments, times, even seasons of your life when God pushed you beyond what was ordinary into the realm of the extraordinary. In today's passage, God is in full creation mode. He is now laying out the design of the planet we now live on. He is emphatically clear there will be levels and dimensions expressed here. That will be waters and that will be land, that will be the sky, and that will be a firmament. It is a design that has been made by God that is absolutely positively flawless. In creation, God sits high and looks low and has all power in his hand. God has created the earth for his glory and the heaven for his place of residence. All of creation reminds us of the splendorous glory of God! It is highly unlikely and seriously improbable for anyone to examine creation and not conclude there is and must be a God. Here's a good devotional question for you to consider today: What proof do you have God actually exists? How do you know there really is a God? The answer is easy: His creation of the earth and everything around us is his résumé and deed of eminent domain! Praise the Lord!

Day 38: And God Said

And God said, "Let the waters under the heaven be gathered together unto one place, and let the dry land appear:", and it was so. (Genesis 1:9)

Our God is an awesome God! Just how awesome is He? Check out the verse listed above. It is a record of creation given on the pages of holy writing describing how God created the universe. Get this; He did not need a shovel, a bulldozer, a crane, or any cement. I heard God is so awesome all He needed to create the entire universe was the words that fell from His mouth! In a very practical sense, God used faith to speak to nothing so that something might exist. Faith in this context is acting like a thing is so, even when it's not so, that it might be so. In short, God declared a thing with his mouth, knowing that what He spoke, He would soon see! When you read the account of creation listed above, your soul should rejoice. The Lord we serve, simply said, "Let that be", and everything in creation responded. The record reflects that the waters under the heavens gather together in one place and the dry land appeared. The blessed news of today is to know God has the power, ability, authority, and the capacity to speak causing things to exist! How would you respond if you were to discover the same faith God used in creation you have access to, every day? Here's the shout of the day: God's modus operandi (mode of operation) is faith, and so is yours. The Bible says the just shall live by faith. The Bible declares that without faith, it is impossible to please God. So walk by faith, not by sight, and expect great things to happen all day long.

Day 39: The Right to Name It And Claim it

And God called the dry land earth; and the gathering together of the waters called he Seas: and God saw that it was good. (Genesis 1:10)

Not long ago, a very popular Pastor did a series on YouTube entitled "Name It and Claim It." During his lesson, he taught people the Bible. It gave Christians the right to name and claim things not been decreed, earned, or purchased. It was viewed by millions of people from around the world. The problem with such teaching is its core is faulty, and its true meaning is often far from what the Lord meant for His people to know and practice. In short, what he was teaching was false, to say the least. When you read verses like the one listed above in our study today. It is safe to conclude there is at least one who has the divinely inspired right to name it and claim it any time He feels like it. Check out the verse listed above. God is naming the earth "dry land." God is naming the waters "seas." God is the one doing the naming; God is the one doing the claiming. He can do both because He has the power, ability, and authority to do so. When the Psalmist looked at the works of the Lord, he declared in Psalms 27 that "The earth was the Lord's and the fullness thereof, the world and they that dwell therein." Because God made it, God reserves the right to call it what He wants to call it because it is His by design and His by way of creation. The celebration found in today's lesson is this: just like God has a right to name and claim creation, He also reserves the right to name and claim you! He made you, and by sovereign rule, you are His, and He is yours.

Day 40: Weeds, Trees and Seeds

And God said, "Let the earth bring forth grass, the herb yielding seed, and the fruit tree yielding fruit after his kind, whose seed is in itself, upon the earth", and it was so. (Genesis 1:11)

There are times when people look at where you are now and assume you have always been where you are. There are times we despise meager beginnings. We don't like starting small and growing large. We like to start big and end bigger. But according to the account of creation given to us in the scriptures, that is not how this thing is designed to work. This passage declares for us that God started with nothing. It further implies when God did begin with the creation, He jumped and started His entire program with grass (weeds), seeds, and trees. Please note: God could have started with monuments reaching the sky and buildings piercing the altitude at amazing heights. But He opted not to do that. God started with weeds, trees, and seeds. The lesson here is enormous. If you start well and God graces it with His favor, where you begin will not be where you wind up! As you read this devotional lesson, ask yourself this question: where did I start? Wait, here's another query to ponder: just how far has the Lord brought me? If you can honestly say, "I have not always had what I have right now," then you understand the bountiful bliss of growth in grace and blessing that comes only when you make progress through a process. Here's the true story: God started with weeds, trees, and seeds. Get started wherever you are. Use what you have and leave the results to the God you love and trust!

Day 41: Watermelons, Peaches and Plums | The Third Day

And the earth brought forth grass and herb yielding seed after his kind, and the tree yielding fruit, whose seed was in itself, after his kind: and God saw that it was good. And the evening and the morning were the third day. (Genesis 1:12-13)

It was a hot summer day in Beaumont; kids at the park were having a blast. Ice-cold bottles of water were going fast, and so were the popsicles and snow cones. When all the cold refreshments ran out, the kids were still in a mode of demanding the most and paying the least. One parent had a trick up her sleeve. She walked over to her trunk and said, "Hey guys, follow me. I have something special for y'all." She arrives at her car, opens the hatch to her SUV, and to the surprise of everyone there, she does not have ice cream, sodas, or even Kool-aid. She had boatloads of fruit on ice. The initial sigh of the kids signaled things would be about to go from bad to worse. But when the kids started eating the plums with juice running down their elbows, devouring those peaches, and biting into the watermelon, the rest was history. When scenes like this come to mind, we should think of passages like the one mentioned above. For God gave us fruit with seeds in them, so we could be blessed by their sweet nectar. God graced us with herb-yielding plants so they would produce after their own kind. You cannot plant oranges and get apples; you cannot sow peaches and get plums. The seed of a thing produces the seed like the thing. This is awesome in every sense of the word, especially when you consider the fact the seeds needed to produce the herb-yielding plants around the world are incalculable and innumerable!

Day 42: Reasons and Seasons

And God said, "Let there be lights in the firmament of the heaven to divide the day from the night; and let them be for signs, and for seasons, and for days, and years". (Genesis 1:14-15)

As the earth rotates on its axis, making its way around the sun, the distance from the sun produces what we know as seasons. The further away from the sun we are, the colder the temperature gets. And the closer we are to the sun, the warmer things get, and everything in between helps us transition between being close and being at a distance to the sun. There are people who just cannot handle cold weather. They shiver when it's sixty degrees outside and collapse when it's thirty or below. Likewise, there are some people who just love hot, humid, steamy weather. They don't mind the heat because they cannot stand the cold. Whatever the case, here's what today's passage teaches us: Every season has a reason. You see, seasons bring signs for days and years. No season comes to stay; and as you watch seasons come and go, not only do the seasons change, you change, too. Hair that was once black turns white; bones that used to move smoothly now come with a snap, crackle, and pop. Why? The answer is simple: Your seasons are changing. The good news about this devotional lesson is God does not stop being God because your season has changed. He is still God; He is there for you in every season of your life. Think about it. Do you remember a season of your life when things were harsh and cold? Wasn't God there for you? When things were warm and wonderful, wasn't He right there? The seasons may change, but God never does!

Day 43: Not Solar Panels, Solar Powered | The Fourth Day

And God made two great lights, the greater light to rule the day, and the lesser light to rule the night. He made the stars, also. And God set them in the firmament of the heaven to give light upon the earth. And God saw that it was good. And the evening and the morning were the fourth day. (Genesis 1:16-19)

Not long ago, a commercial surfaced on YouTube television marketing newly designed solar panels. They were designed to reduce your light bill by as much as $300.00 a month. There is no more need for electricity, because the solar panels would do the trick. The brochure attached to the advertisement made it clear that as long as the earth had sunshine, you would never need an electric company again. When we pause to consider such things, we have to be mindful that God is the great creator of not just solar panels; He is the progenitor of solar power! Your God made the sun and gave it a right to shine and it hasn't stopped shining yet. This passage tells us the true story of two great lights: The Sun and the Moon. It declares for us the story of tiny, small lights that we look into the heavens and declare to be stars. The benefit of having these cosmic lights is not that they help us transform what would be night into the bliss of day. It is much more than that. They help us to remember God made those lights, and without Him, we would be trapped in everlasting darkness. What way is God a light in your life? What does it mean for Jesus to be the light of the world to you? Don't forget this bit of wisdom and truth: You will never walk in darkness as long as you have the light of life walking with you. `

Day 44: No Tickets Needed For the Zoo or the Aquarium

And God said, "Let the waters bring forth abundantly the moving creature that hath life, and fowl that may fly above the earth in the open firmament of heaven." And God created great whales and every living creature that moveith, which the waters brought forth abundantly, after their kind, and every winged fowl after his kind: and God saw that it was good. (Genesis 1:20-21)

The city of Houston, Texas, has the most marvelous zoo and aquarium ever. The animals are amazing; the sea creatures are breathtaking. But the ticket prices are astronomical. However, when it comes to the work of the Lord and the creation of all that we have been blessed with, both the animals and sea creatures are here for our benefit and blessing. Here's the true story of the passage: God created birds of the air and the creatures of the sea. The word "created" used in this passage is Asha. It means to make from existing material. God took water and made whales with it. He took different types of matter and made birds of the air. When God looked at what He created, it was as if He was a spectator of His own work. He examined it, saying it was good. Here's the blessing of today's lesson: God is a God of variety! No fish in the sea is the same. No bird in the air is a replica of the other. Each species is different; each type of mammal in the water is a witness to the fact that if God makes something different, it is supposed to stand out. In short, a bass is not a trout; a dove is not an eagle, and a horse is not a mule. But each one of God's marvelous creations has at least one thing in common: they can all boast they were made by God for our good and His glory!

Day 45: Not Preservation, But Population | The Fifth Day

And God blessed them, saying, "Be fruitful, and multiply, and fill the waters of the seas, and let the fowl multiply in the earth." And the evening and the morning were the fifth day. (Genesis 1:22-23)

The Animal Planet is a wonderful educational documentary on wildlife around the world. It highlights what animals do in their native habitat. It monitors and measures their activities, which can range from mating and reproduction, to feeding and the need to survive. Not long ago, there was a segment aired that gave great attention to how animal preservationists have been instrumental in saving certain species from becoming extinct. Have you ever seen programs like this? They are viewed by millions of people. Yet, when you read the scriptures, the command coming from God in creation was not preservation, but population. Just as the Lord commanded these wonderful creatures be made, He also commanded they "multiply." This one term is used over and in the creation story. It literally means there should be a population by means of replication. The difference here in this passage is that preservation is the effort of humankind to keep a certain species alive. But, population is the favor of God. Upon which a species is graced by God who says, "I'm not through with your kind just yet, so I will just favor you to keep on, keeping on until I decide otherwise." You know, the same grace animals need to survive is the same grace we need to remain alive just another day. If you are alive right now, it is because God wants you here!

Day 46: The Original Cattle Company

And God said, "Let the earth bring forth the living creature after his kind, cattle, and creeping thing", and God saw that it was good. (Genesis 1:24-25)

Are you one of those people who refuse to eat meat? If so, you may not find this entry insightful. However, if you do eat meat, then you can say "Amen" to the steaks the Cattle Company can cook up. They are simply the best! However, when you read the sign marketing the restaurant's logo, it needs to be corrected. It reads, "The Original Cattle Company." Based on the tenets and truths of scripture, a sign like that is false advertising. Here's a true story: God is the founder, leader, and CEO of the Original Cattle Company. When you read the sacred sentiments of this passage, it declares for us that our God put the cow on four legs, made him eat green grass, and gave him white milk. God made the beasts of the field to be carnivorous and herbivorous; He made some to move fast while other beasts moved like frozen honey on a cold winter morning. God made every beast of the field, so the claim to be the Original Cattle Company belongs to Him. The Psalmist agrees with this contention when he writes that our God is the owner of the cattle of a thousand hills. Here's what He means: Whenever you see a cow or any beast of the field, its rightful owner is not the people who branded him, but the God who created him. So the next time you find yourself with a nice juicy ribeye on your plate, you should not just thank God for the steak, but praise God for the animal that was sacrificed so you could live. And, remember, the ultimate sacrifice of our Lamb at the cross!

Day 47: It Was a Masterpiece

And God said, "Let us make man in our image, after our likeness: and let them have dominion. So God created man in His own image, in the image of God created him: Male and Female created He them. (Genesis 1:26-27)

Take a moment today and read the creation story written in Genesis 1:1-27. Read it carefully. Look at it like you're a private investigator looking for clues that just might unravel one of the greatest mysteries of all time. Read the passage like you are trying to figure out why humankind is God's masterpiece of creation. Have you completed your reading assignment yet? If you have not, please do. If you have, check this observation out. It is going to bless you like crazy. Notice when God creates something during the creative process. Whatever He speaks to becomes the source of what He just created. For example, when God wanted fish, He spoke to the sea. Thus, the sea is the source of all fish. If you remove a fish from the water, it dies. When God wanted a cow, He spoke to the earth. So, if you remove a cow from the earth, it dies. When God wanted trees, He spoke to the ground. If you remove a tree from the ground, it dies. But when God created man, He did not speak to the sea, the earth, or even the sky. God spoke to Himself! This means without God, we die. Wait, now here's the shout of the day: The source of creation contains the potential of what has been created. A fish has the potential to govern the sea. An animal has the potential to govern the land. But mankind has been made in the image of God our potential is to operate and dwell as God dwells. It is what we are called to have dominion! No other creature in creation has dominion, but you do! In short, God says when the earth looks at you; "I want them to think about me." It is why, when God created you, it was a masterpiece!

Day 48: I'm Leaving You in Charge

And God blessed them, and God said unto them, be fruitful, and multiply, and replenish the earth, and subdue it. And have dominion over the fish of the sea and over the fowl of the air and over every living thing that moveith upon the earth. (Genesis 1:28)

Just a few years ago, parents who had more than one child did not hire a babysitter to watch their younger siblings. Of course, in our current culture, we hire people who are trained and equipped to watch our children, when adults are not present. Such was not the case just a few years ago. Here's how it came to happen. When an adult had to go to work and did not make enough money to pay a baby sister, they would not hire someone to guide, guard, and govern their behavior. The oldest child would be deputized by their mother with words and instructions like these, "Take care of this house, go to bed at 9:00 pm, and remember, I'm leaving you in charge!" Here's the true story of humankind. When you look at the state of our world, keep in mind. God created everything; he then created mankind and gave both males and females some very keen, clear, and complete instructions: I'm leaving you in charge! This means what our world looks like is not God's fault at all. It is the result of decisions human choice has made. God left us in charge, and just like Adam and Eve made a mess in the Garden of Eden, we, too, have made a mess of the world we live in. We have left God out, put faith in our flesh, and have made decisions to do life for our own good and not the glory of God. Our one saving grace that should cause every Christian not to lose hope: God has never given up on us! He has never changed His mind on His most marvelous creation...Humankind.

Day 49: I've Got It All | The Sixth Day

And God said, behold, I have given you every herb bearing seed, which is upon the face of all the earth. And every tree, in which is the fruit of a tree yielding seed. To you it shall be for meat. And every beast of the earth and to every fowl of the air, and to everything that creepeth upon the earth. Wherein there is life, I have given every green herb for meat: and it was so. (Genesis 1:29-30)

The story was told of a ten-year-old boy standing in line at Target. His basket was filled with toys and games, clothes and shoes. The line was long; the wait seemingly took forever. A gentleman standing behind this ten-year-old asked him why he had so many toys. He replied, "Today is my birthday. I'm ten-years-old today!" The kind man then asked, "Well, what do you have in your basket?" To which the ten-year-old said, "Looking at all of my stuff, I can say, 'I've got it all!'" When you consider everything the Lord bestowed upon humankind in creation, we too can say, as the ten-year-old kid said, "I've got it all!" Yes, the earth belongs to the Lord. By this, it means it is His because He made it. Yet the earth belongs to humankind because the God of creation deeded it. In short, God deeded it to us! Every tree, every seed, every bird, every fowl, every beast that runs, every beast that walks, every fish that swims, and everything that creeps. God made it, and the Lord gave us to work it and keep it. Here's the truth of the sixth day of creation: God blessed us with it. We have it all!

Day 50: It's All Good

Good…good…good…good…good…good…Good (Genesis 1:4b, 10b 12b, 18b, 21b, 25b, and 31b)

Here's an absolutely true fact: God is good! In fact, God created matter, time, and space. When He finished, He declared it to be good. Think of it this way: If there is a shoe, there has to be a shoemaker. If there is a shirt, there is a shirt maker. If there is a car, there must be a carmaker. And if there is a suit, there has to be a suit maker. With this philosophy in mind, if there is a galaxy, there must be a galaxy maker. If there is earth, there must be an earth producer. If there is a sun, there has to be a sun builder. And if there is a moon, there has to be a moon designer and developer, somewhere! When you read the account of creation given in Genesis 1, there is a pattern running through the narrative like a crimson cord through a white quilt. It is the declaration that God says over and over what He created was good! In fact, God declared everything He made was good. Do you want to know why He knows it is good? Here's the answer, and it should truly bless you. It is good because He made it! In short, God does not make trash. If God made it, the assurance of it being good is one hundred percent guaranteed. Take a look in the mirror, as you start your day, today, whisper these words to yourself. They should empower, enlighten, and encourage you: IT'S ALL GOOD!

Day 51: Take A Chill Pill for Just A Minute | The Seventh Day

Thus, the heavens and the earth were finished, and all the hosts of them. And on the seventh day, God ended the work he had made, and he rested on the seventh day from all the work he had done. And God blessed the seventh day, and sanctified it: because that in it he had rested from all his work, which God created and made. (Genesis 2:1-3)

Have you ever worked for a while and just needed to rest? Have you ever labored long enough to say to yourself, "I'm taking a break not because I need one, but because I deserve one?" If you can say yes, then you can feel the pulse of the passage listed above. It is exactly what took place on Day 7 of creation. Now, here's the shout: It's not that God got tired of working. He has all the power and never needs a break; however, He had worked long enough to deserve one. So He took a break and called it the Sabbath. In modern lingo, we would say God said, "I'm gonna take a chill pill for a minute." We rest because we need it. God rests because He defines it. We rest because we get worn out. God rests because He decides to call timeout. With this in mind, when was the last time you took a chill pill and rested for a moment? If you haven't lately, now may be a good time to take one. You deserve it!

Day 52: When God Plays Patty-Cake

And the Lord God formed man of the dust of the ground, and breathed into his nostrils the breath of life; and man became a living soul. (Genesis 2:7)

It was a game children played years ago. It was an outdoor game requiring a little dirt, some water, and some ingenious creative artwork. It was a game known as Patty-Cake. A few years ago, most of the games children played were outdoor games. Patty-Cake was just one of them. Here's what happened when you played. You would take some dirt, molding it with your hands until it became what you want it to be. Usually, it came out looking like a pancake made from mud. Now shift gears with your mind and imagine for a moment what would happen if God played a little Patty-Cake Himself. For the really deep saint, this may sound like complete foolishness. However, for those who can see it with a clear mind, it's what happened when God made man. Our God took a hand full of dirt and molded it with His hands until it became what He wanted it to be! With this in mind, we could safely say we have been handmade by the Creator Himself. Here's the celebration: When God finished making you, He destroyed the design, so there will never be another just like you!!

Day 53: A Dream Home

And the Lord God planted a garden eastward in Eden, and there he put the man whom he had formed. And the Lord God made to grow every tree that is pleasant to the sight and good for food. The tree of life was also in the midst of the Garden, and the tree of knowledge of good and evil. And a river went out of Eden to water the Garden, and from thence it was parted and became into four heads. (Genesis 2:8-10)

What does your dream home look like, perhaps, a beautiful modern six-bedroom palace with a glass foyer in the front, a gorgeous pool and cabana outback? Maybe even a nice country colonial-style house with a front porch with freshly painted rocking chairs, and a lake loaded with catfish outback? What does it look like? Well, while you consider what your dream home would look like, check out the description of the dream home God constructed for Adam and Eve. They had a ceiling; they had the picturesque beauty of a clear blue sky. They didn't have chandeliers made in Italy; God graced them with the effervescent glory of the sun during the day to be accompanied by the moon and the stars at night. They didn't have carpet, they were given plush green grass filled with floral arrangements God made just for them. And did you say a Jacuzzi tub? Not good enough! God graced them with the smooth streams of the Nile River, the warm rushing water of the Pihon, and the seas of the earth just to enjoy. It was beauty beyond the decree. Wait, did you ask how many square feet this dwelling was? Try to swallow this; it was the circumference of the earth and the width of the galaxy! It wasn't their dream home; it was God's dream for them to have! Keep this in mind: As long as you live, God wants to bless you, and for you to have the best. It's why He gave us Himself in Jesus Christ!

Day 54: There's Gold in Them There Hills

The name of the first is Pison: that is it which compasseth the whole land of Havilah, where there is gold. And the gold of that land is good: there is bdellium and the onyx stone. (Genesis 2:11-12)

People often refer to the United States of America as the land of opportunity. And often, this is absolutely true. The freedoms we enjoy in our system of both democracy and capitalism are like none other. Yet, when you open a Bible and peruse the true story of how the Lord, in creation, blessed Adam and Eve, things take a turn for the greater. You see, the Lord sat in the Garden of Eden in a region where there was water and vegetation. Not only was the water from existing rivers, there were minerals buried in the soil there that would give them a degree of wealth and blessings for generations to come. Here's how the passage puts it: ... whole land of Havilah where there is gold; and the gold of that land is good." A better translation of this periscope would be to say God positioned Adam in a place where he would say, "There's gold in them there hills!" The bonifide blessing for us to rejoice about is this: You do not put people near gold if you want them to remain in poverty. It was God's intent for Adam to have the same gold! Wait, the man had to work to get it. The gold did not just leap onto his shovel and into his proverbial bank account. He had to labor to get it. The blessing for us is it was there all the time. What if you discovered the same God who blessed Adam and Eve wants to do the same thing for you, too? The gold was a gift of grace from God to His creation. Praise the Lord for gold, which is good!

Day 55: Check Out the Backyard

And the name of the second river is Gihon, the same is it that compasseth the whole land of Ethiopia. And the name of the third river is Hiddekel; that is it which goeth toward the east of Assyria. And the fourth river is Euphrates. (Genesis 2:13-14)

A local real estate agent recently posted an amazing story on social media. He stated he had a customer looking for a special home in the city. His budget was a mere $750,000.00. In Beaumont, Texas, a house like that is really made for the rich and famous. It would be the equivalent of a home in Los Angeles costing about $20,000,000.00! The crazy part about this true story was his housing hunter only wanted to see the backyard of every home. The shopper did not care to see the master bedroom, the kitchen, the foyer, not even the family room. He only looked at backyards. When asked why, he replied, "A backyard tells you what the character of the house is really like." If what he stated was true, the character of the Garden of Eden was not just one of a kind; it was godly. Reread the passage listed above and imagine what you are reading being the backyard of Adam and Even. Can you see it? Can you imagine it? If you do not gain anything else from today's entry, remember this: God never half does anything, not even a backyard designed for just two people. Quick question: Has God ever blessed you above and beyond measure? What did He do? Here's the shout: It's not like you earned it. He just decided to graciously do it!

Day 56: Handle Your Business

And the Lord God took the man and put him into the Garden of Eden to dress it and to keep it. (Genesis 2:15)

"Get to work!" These are the words parents used to exclaim with vigor for people who were raised old school. There was no such thing as a dirty house with kids sitting around the home front. If you were a young man, this command was even more forceful. This was not some mark of sexism to such that girls were not supposed to work, but it was nearly impossible for a young man to be lazy, shiftless, and not willing to work. And, from the looks of our passage shared above, God feels the same way. In fact, the first assignment a man ever had in the scriptures was to go to work! Yes, the place where Adam lived was paradise, literally. His job was to dress it and keep it. In other words, God graced him with it, but Adam was still responsible and accountable for what took place in it. When the Lord finished with the Garden, it was as if He had just said, "Adam, handle your business!" In short, God gave Adam a job. You see, with work comes moments of discovery, discipline, and definition. With work come endurance, perseverance, and inheritance. Work is godly and is of God!

Day 57: Hook a Brotha Up Then

And the Lord God said, "It is not good that the man should be alone; I will make him a helper for him. (Genesis 2:18)

There is something wrong with any man who cannot appreciate and applaud the divinity expressed by God in the creation of femininity. In short, there is something so special about a woman God Himself waited to create her just so He could outdo Himself. Here's the true story revealed in this passage: Nothing God created was designed for a man to be compatible with. The giraffe was too tall, the hippo was too mean, the monkey played too much, and the lioness was not having it. So God decided to "Hook a brotha up." God literally made a sovereign decision to make a species just to complement a man. God makes *a helper for him*. The emphasis here in Hebrew is so rich. It should read like this, "I will make a companion tailor-made for him." The word "make" used in this passage is Asha. It means to make something from material that already exists. Please note, when God decides to make a helper for man, it does not include man's advice or input. In short, a woman is God's gift to a real man who knows what she is, who she is, and how to treat her. She is God's favor expressed to manhood for the purpose of being purposefully connected to him. Praise the Lord for womanhood!

Day 58: Big Baller, Shot Caller

And out of the ground the Lord God formed every beast of the field and every fowl of the air. He brought them unto Adam to see what he would call them, and whatsoever Adam called every living creature that was the name thereof. And Adam gave names to all cattle and to the fowl of the air and to every beast of the field; but for Adam there was not found a helper for him. (Genesis 2:19-20)

Have you ever wondered how the cheetah got its name or how the lion, being the king of the jungle, got its title? Well, wonder no more. God empowered Adam in the Garden with the authority and the ability to name everything He had created. In fact, the true story revealed above lets us know whatever Adam called creation is what the Lord called them. There is a great deal of authority expressed in this passage. To name something is to give you the right to be superior to what you are named. In this, God makes it known Adam is His "Big Baller, Shot Caller." The man that God made stood above, beyond, and over everything that had been designed by the Lord. Adam, the man, has no equal to make his rivalry on earth. Nothing compares to him, and God wants that known. The blessing of this passage is to paint a picture of God's man that says, "He's responsible, and I want everyone to know it, including him." Do you have children? You named them. Do you have a pet? If so, you named them, too. Now imagine having the privilege, the fortitude, aptitude, magnitude, and ability to name all creation! That's what God did for Adam!

Day 59: The Surgery Went Well

And the Lord God caused a deep sleep to fall upon Adam, and he slept. And he took one of his ribs, closing up the flesh instead thereof; and the rib, which the Lord God had taken from man, made He a woman, and brought her unto the man. (Genesis 2:21-22)

History records the first took place in about 6,500 BC. The procedure was called trepanation. It was a small hole drilled in the back of the head by a hammer and sharp device. It was believed back then this surgery would cure migraine headaches. Thank God for Aleve, right? However this story may be a fact, but it is not the truth. Here's the true story about the first surgery; it took place in the Garden of Eden. When it was time for God to actually make a mate for Adam, He ".....caused a deep sleep to fall upon Adam and He took one of His ribs and....made he a woman...." This may sound crazy, but it's the truth. Now, here's the shout: God did not use any anesthesia; He didn't need a scalpel, a lazar, or even an assist to look over His shoulder. He did not require a sterilized environment to work in. Why? The Holiness He wore as a cloak and the glory He carries with Him everywhere He goes, purged the area. And the record reflects the good news of the moment would sound like this after it was all over: The surgery went well! Has God ever held your hand and walked you through a procedure before? If you came out of it and lived to tell about it, thank God the surgery went well!

Day 60: A Real Man Loves a Rib

And Adam said, "This is now bone of my bones, and flesh of my flesh: she shall be called woman, because she was taken out of Man." (Genesis 2:23)

Broussard's Bar-B-Que is a community staple in Beaumont, Texas. It's located on the corner of Washington Boulevard and 11th Street in a section of the town called the Pear Orchid. For almost a half-century, it's been known for its homemade links, secret sauce, and ribs. One day, while opening a hot pan of these Broussard's specialties, a young man exclaimed with vigor, "I can pass on the chicken 'cause a real man loves a rib." Even though he was referring to a rib from a restaurant, it is the feel of the passage listed above. When Adam first looked at Eve, he rose from surgery in the recovery room, he declared, "She is bone of my bones and flesh of my flesh." Adam loved what he saw and came to grips with the fact a real man loves a rib! There's a saying suggesting that "Behind every good man stands a good woman." But this could not be further from the truth. Here's the true story: The woman was taken from the side of a man, and that is where she belongs: not behind him, but right by his side.

Day 61: The Rule Is - Leave and Cleave

Therefore shall a man leave his father and his mother, and shall cleave unto his wife: and they shall be one flesh. (Genesis 2:24)

Marriages in our current day struggle, like never before. Men quit on their families, weekly, and women call it quits all the time. One of the many problems causing this marital collapse is the ruin of third-party intrusions; the presence of in-laws who can behave like outlaws. They're so-called friends with horrid, horrible, unholy advice. People are making comments that exist from the outside in and have a negative effect on the relationship inside. When all is finished, it is making family practice lawyers wealthy, keeping the judge's chambers busy, forcing the state to demand child support payments, and the hurt goes on. There's a bit of marital counseling found here in the creation story that is true and powerful. It's a simple rule; when followed it works. Here it is for your consideration: "Leave and Cleave." It means to "Release and Retain." In short, get to a place where nothing can separate a husband from his wife and a wife from her husband, putting God in their midst. At the moment this takes place, the question is not if they can survive; the truth of is they will survive; because God cannot and will not fail them. Marriage still works when you "Leave and Cleave."

Day 62: Naked and Not Ashamed

Therefore shall a man leave his father and his mother, and shall cleave unto his wife: and they shall be one flesh. (Genesis 2:25)

Have you ever been involved in a relationship that made you feel vulnerable? Have you ever loved someone to the point you felt weak, silly, and frail? Have you had a case of the "can't help it?" Just for those who have never had a case of the "can't help it," it normally takes place when you can't help but love someone. Even in times when you do not like their actions towards you or others. It brings you to a place of being naked before them and not ashamed of it. Here's the truth about today's story: Adam and Eve lived in a period called innocence. They knew no sin. They knew no wrong. They knew nothing of disobedience. They had never been introduced to lying, cheating, pride, arrogance, or rebellion. They had no idea what it was like to fail and needed grace to take their place. They were completely naked and not ashamed. The celebration of this lesson is they had no reason to be ashamed because they were completely mistake-free before the Lord our God. Think about this for a moment: how many of your secret sins do you hope will never be discovered? How many times have you become a cover-up artist because you are ashamed of what you have done and the mistakes you have made? Here's a radical truth: You can hide from people and run for cover, before God, you are naked because He can see who and what you really are, and He still loves you! It's where Adam and Eve were in our true story today: Naked and Not Ashamed.

THE STORY OF CHAOS IN PARADISE

Day 63: When Your Snakes Have Legs

Now the serpent was cleverer than any beast of the field, which the Lord God had made. And he said unto the woman, "Yea, hath God said, 'Ye shall not eat of every tree of the garden?'" (Genesis 3:1)

This may come as a surprise to some of you; there are some snakes that have legs. They hiss all the time; threaten to strike from time to time and when worse comes to worse they even bite, doing damage beyond decree. The true story of our record in Genesis is that when the serpent approached Eve in the Garden of Eden he was not crawling, the serpent was walking. We know this because after he is cursed by God he is told he would crawl on the ground for the remainder of his time on earth. The passage listed about presents the serpent walking into the Garden and subtly approaching Eve with lies, deceit, and deception. It's a true story every believer should never forget. And, here's why; just like Eve was approached by a snake with legs, there are times you are challenged with your own horrible huddle of snakes. They are people who mean you harm and not good; folks who seek to rob you of your potential; kill your dreams; dash your hopes and if you let them, they will bring you down. But, keep this in mind; you will never beat a snake, being a snake! Your only hope is to leave them in the dust they came in and rise above them!

Day 64: To know what's Right Is One Thing, To Do It Is Another

And the woman said unto the serpent, "We may eat of the fruit of the trees of the garden. But of the fruit of the tree which is in the midst of the garden, God hath said, 'Ye shall not eat of it; neither shall ye touch it, lest ye die.'" (Genesis 3:2-3)

Have you ever known what's right and chose wrong? Have you ever had a moment in your life where you knew better, but did not do better? Have you ever been privy to godly principle, but failed miserably? If you have then heard this, you are not alone. Eve is in your amen corner at this very moment. In today's passage Eve is not only totally aware of the instructions and directions from the Lord, but she even adds the phrase "…neither shall we touch it, lest we die." It is a resounding truth she is aware of what God expects. However, in this true story what she knows and what she does don't line up quite right. By this is meant, she knows what the Lord has told her today; yet her struggle is real enough to know the instructions and miss the application by a long shot. One commentary writer said that when he saw Eve in heaven he was going to kick her in the knee. But, here's something else to consider: Where was Adam while this conversation was going on? It stands to reason; if Adam was close enough to hear the conversation he should have been man enough to put this smooth talking snake in his place. The bottom line here is this: To know better is one thing; to do it is another. Here's a solid devotional word of wisdom for you to consider: Make a decision to do the right thing. And, when you make your decision clear, your decision will make other decisions for you!

Day 65: He's Such a Liar

And the serpent said unto the woman, "Ye shall not surely die." (Genesis 3:4)

So here's a true story I hope you never forget it. The devil is a liar! He lies to you, he lies about you; he will soon stand before God and lie on you. He is a liar! He lies about God's plan for your life. He lies about what God has said and what you should believe. He lies about why you should doubt God; he even lies about the lies he tells. Be careful. He is smooth, charismatic, warm, compassionate and easy to follow. But if you fall prey to his evil plots and plans, he will try to convince you God is not good, He should not be trusted and he certainly should not be worshipped, followed, or prayed to. While lecturing one day on the subject of Christian Education, Dr. Jonathan C. Jackson made this observation, "Our enemy is such a liar he lies even when he is trying to tell the truth." The lies he shares above rest and remains in the fact he knows he is lying and lies any way. Here the serpent tells Eve, "….ye shall not surely die." This is a total lie! Have you ever been lied to? How did you feel? Have you ever lied to someone and it proved to be crushing? God despises a liar because when we lie we are most like Satan and when we share the truth and declare it, we are most like God!

Day 66: Trickery, Treachery and Deceit

For God doth know that in the day ye eat thereof, then your eyes shall be opened, and ye shall be as gods, knowing good and evil. (Genesis 3:5)

There's a difference between trickery, treachery and deceit even though they are fruit that fall from the same tree. Trickery is a lie designed by the user to gain a favored outcome by being slick. Treachery is a lie presented, but carries an inherent desire to harm the person towards whom the lies have been told. And, deceit is best defined as the skillful use of words presented by a liar that can show you one thing but do something totally different. But, what do you know when one agent contains and uses all three of these vices at one time against you? That's the tension of the text listed above. The enemy presented in the passage tricks Eve into doing what God says not to do. His treachery is seen because the same God that expelled him out of the Lord's presence will be the same God that administers judgment on Eve for being disobedient and he is a deceiver. Keep this in mind, the best lie to tell is a false statement with a little deceit mixed in it. This is the kind of lie the devil uses and continues to use. Take a moment; look closely at your life and your walk with God. Have you ever had a moment when the deceiver tricked you? Have you ever fallen for one of his lies? How did you overcome the trouble it caused you? Don't let any of the enemy's trickery, treachery, and deceit work on you. Stand for the truth of God's Word and He will always put you in a place of victory!

Day 67: It's Been Declared a Disaster Area

And when the woman saw that the tree was good for food, and that it was pleasant to the eyes, and a tree to be desired to make one wise, she took of the fruit thereof. And she did eat, and gave also unto her husband with her; and he did eat. (Genesis 3:6)

Jefferson County, Texas is a costal region sitting on the lip of the Gulf Mexico. The Gulf is 443 quadrillion gallons of water. When hurricanes come ashore, packing category three wind speeds and higher it is normal for the State and the Federal government to declare the entire region a disaster area. By doing this, what the county and state leaders are saying is the damage is so extensive it cannot be repaired with help that's external. When you look at the story in today's passage, it should not be shocking that God declared it to be a disaster area. Here's how the true story goes. Eve swaps personal observation for obedience. She thinks the tree is good for good. She falls prey to what it looks like instead of judging forbidden fruit for what it was, and she did not read the fine print in the contract. The fruit would make her wise like god, but Eve forgot to check the spelling: it was a lowercase god and not a capital God! The end result is chaos in paradise. All hell breaks loose. To add insult to injury, Adam eats willing, though Eve has been deceived. The good news is even though a Disaster Area can be declared; help is always on the way! Even though damage has been done, the fight is not over yet because there's some relief coming that will take what is damaged and claimed to be a disaster and completely restore. Here's a good question for you: Have you ever seen God restore a disaster before? He has done it, He can do it, and He will do it again!

Day 68: The Great Cover-Up

And the eyes of them both were opened, and they knew that they were naked; and they sewed fig leaves together, and made themselves aprons. (Genesis 3:7)

Did you know after Adam and Eve had eaten of the forbidden fruit they both realized they were naked? Do you know what happened to them next? They did what any of us would do, which is trying to deal with our human failures and secret flaws. They took fig leaves and stitched them together for the purpose of covering it up. In short, it was the beginning of the great cover-up. It is where guilt and shame collide. You do understand guilt is internal and shame is external. Guilt is where you know you have made a mess of things, except nobody knows it. Shame is when you messed it up, but it is now public knowledge. When moments like this happen, we run for shelter and seek cover. Has it ever happened to you? The story was told of a little boy who wanted to go berry picking, but his father told him he could not go. However, his three so-called friends convinced him to do otherwise. After all, his father was at work so he wouldn't know he ever left the house. They go berry picking and come back with buckets of berries and then a huge problem surfaced. His father came home early from work. The little boy walked into the house; his father asked him, "Where have you been? Have you been picking berries?" The little boy said "no dad." As he turned around to walk away, he had blueberry stains all over the back of his pants. You see, his cover-up went well until he missed spots on his rear end. Here's the moral of today's lesson: Cover-up's somehow end up busted up and will need grace to cover them.

Day 69: Trust Me, This Ain't Hide And Go Seek

And they heard the voice of the Lord God walking in the garden in the cool of the day. And Adam and his wife hid themselves from the presence of the Lord God amongst the trees of the garden. (Genesis 3:8)

Hide and go seek was a childhood game played by kids reared in the 70's and 80's. The whole purpose to winning the game was to hide and find a way to make it home without getting caught. Have you ever played it before? Back then it was fun and games. But, what we have in this passage is anything but fun and it certainly is not a game. Here's a question you should think about after reading a passage like the one mentioned above. Where do you run after you have made a mistake? What do you do when you fail, falter and fall flat on your face? Here's what normally happens: we run and hide. Trust this statement, "It ain't hide and go seek." You see, the truth about today's story is the fact that after Adam and Eve missed the mark in the Garden they hid themselves from the presence of the Lord. Quick devotional question: Have you ever wanted to just hide before? If you can answer yes, you know how Adam and Eve felt. They did not want to be seen. They did not want to be heard. They wanted to hide completely out of sight. The presence of sin brings a sincere heart to repentance every time! You feel so low, empty, void, silly, stupid and lost. The good news about such a feeling is when you are low, that's when God can lift you up and graciously help you start again. God is a redemptionist who yearns to lift you from your hiding place and set your life on a pedal so everyone can see what grace truly looks like.

Day 70: Adam, Why Are You Where You Are?

And the Lord God called unto Adam, and said unto him, "Where art thou?" (Genesis 3:9)

So after Adam and Eve realized they made a huge mistake they sought to cover their naked condition with aprons made of fig leaves and they hid behind some bushes. The Lord God comes walking through the Garden in the cool of the day and poses this question you find in the passage listed above, "Adam, where are thou?" It should be understood this is not a question of Adam's location. Keep this in mind, it is God walking through the Garden and God knows everything. He knows where Adam is. This is a query that carries a much deeper overtone. It is a question of Adams' disposition. It could be better asked like this, "Why are you where you are?" You see, when the Lord left the Garden Adam was left with dominion and power; authority and strength; position and a title. Yet when the Lord observes what is in the Garden, now, the same man He blessed is hiding behind some bushes because he's naked. If you've been reading the lessons leading up to this point, you should know how Adam got into this predicament. But, just in case you missed it, Adam and Eve did exactly what God commanded them not to do. And, the end result is a question that presses everyone to answer it at some point in life's journey. Here's the question: Why are you where you are? Ponder it. Pray on it. Be honest and transparent with yourself. A truthful answer could explain a great deal that has taken place in your life.

Day 71: Naked and Ashamed

And he said, "I heard thy voice in the garden, and I was afraid, because I was naked; and I hid myself." (Genesis 3:10)

Take a moment; revisit the entry made on Day 62. It is entitled "Naked and Not Ashamed." Now look carefully at this verse and its title. Can you see the difference? Can you feel the failure? Just in case you can't feel anything, here is what is happening in the story given in passages. On Day 62 Adam and Eve are naked and living in paradise and blessed beyond measure with the earth under their feet, the sky as their limit and one tree they cannot eat from. Suddenly in this passage, the story has reversed itself. They are not aware of their nakedness, ashamed about their condition and have sought to cover it up and instead of enjoying the greenery; they are now hiding behind the shrubbery. What on earth happened you ask? Sin! Though the word sin is not mentioned in this passage at all, this is exactly what it is. Sin! It is an ugly, unruly, unscrupulous term meaning someone had the unmitigated guts to tell God no! Sin! It means to miss the mark. Sin! It means to know what God said and do the exact opposite of it, knowing there will be consequences. Sin! It is what brings both guilt and shame. Often when we think about sin we think of the faults and failures of others. Rarely do we look at ourselves and say "God please work on me." But today should be different. Think of sins, which should make you hide from the Lord: pride, lying, hatred, sexual misconduct, lust, disobedience, rebellion, and maybe even ungratefulness. Whatever your sin is, don't hide from God, run to Him! He's waiting on you and He can handle

Day 72: When God Has Questions for You

And he said, "Who told thee that thou wast naked? Hast thou eaten of the tree, whereof I commanded thee that thou shouldest not eat?" (Genesis 3:11)

Have you ever reached a point in your life where you had questions for God? Questions like "Lord, why me?" And, what about this question when you find yourself tired of waiting, "God, how long?" Let's set the record straight, life will bring you to a place where you will look up into the heavens and ask God questions only He can answer. But, here's the true story for today found in the passage listed above. Just like you have questions for God, there are times God has questions for you! It's what happened in the Garden of Eden after Adam and Eve missed the mark. God showed up and posed three questions needed to be answered. Question number one: "Where are you?" This is a question of disposition and should be rendered like this, "Why are you in the condition you are in?" Question number two: "Who told you that you were naked?" In other words, "Why in the world would you listen to anyone other than me?" In other words the Lord says "You have been naked the whole time and that was never a problem for me. My issue right now is who have you been listening to other than me?" Question number three: "Hast thou eaten?" A better way to interpret this questioning is to ask "Have you done what I instructed you not to do?" As you spend this moment today in devotional study, you should ask yourself these same questions. The good news is God already knows the answers. The blessed news is once you are honest about each of them restoration is on the way.

Day 73: And The Blame Game Begins

And the man said, "The woman whom thou gavest to be with me, she gave me of the tree, and I did eat." (Genesis 3:12)

The story was told of a little girl who got in trouble at school for acting out and cutting up. She was so bad; the principal called her parents and asked them to come get her from school early. When they got her home, love and discipline were on the horizon for her. Just before the discipline took place, her mother asked her why she behaved so poorly at school; she said, "It's not my fault; it all started with the girl sitting behind me!" It's the game we play when we do not want to face judgment, wrath or punishment. It is the excuse we use for the human condition; bad decision making, and human mistakes. When a team loses the coach blames the referees, the players blame one another, and the guy who missed the last shot becomes the fall guy for the entire loss. However, the truth of the matter is no one wants to face the hurt of losing, so we blame the three celebrity personalities known for enduring such moments. We blame anybody, somebody, and everybody because we cannot possibly be the problem. Here in this true story: Adam blamed Eve; Eve blamed the serpent and the snake admitted he was just being a snake. Take a moment to ask yourself these questions once more: Whose fault is it you're in the condition you're in? Who have you been listening to who misled you? Why have you made some of the decisions you made? When questions like these are raised, a shift towards the positive takes place; when we answer without blaming anyone and accepting responsibility for ourselves.

Day 74: Girl, What In the World Have You Done

And the Lord God said unto the woman, "What is this that thou hast done?" And the woman said, "The serpent beguiled me, and I did eat." (Genesis 3:13)

So here's the story. When the blame game started the Lord looked at Eve and said "What is this thou hast done?" However, it sounds like King James talking when you read it like that. For you to sense and recognize the severity of the matter, this question is better phrased like this, "Girl, what in the world have you done?" It is a moment of personal confrontation. It is piercing and painful. It is hurtful and embarrassing. It puts you on the witness stand knowing the guilt you wear has been earned and not given. For the purpose of storytelling, Eve was deceived. She was tricked. The term used "beguiled" comes from a Hebrew term meaning to be slapped in the dark. Eve blames the serpent and says "That snake over there sucker punched me." Yes, it is true Adam ate of the fruit knowingly and willingly. However, it should not go without notice Adam was close enough to take a bite of fruit. If this is true, he was also close enough to hear the conversation he had with Eve. So Adam's silence could be looked upon as consent. No matter how it is measured, Eve is confronted because she messed the whole thing up, big time! Okay, it's time for a moment of complete honesty. Has the devil ever sucker punched you? Has he ever slapped you in the dark and made you feel foolish? If you answered yes then you too know how Eve must have felt when in the Lord's presence in this passage.

Day 75: The First Curse Didn't Come From the Devil

And the Lord God said unto the serpent, "Because thou hast done this, thou art cursed above all cattle, and above every beast of the field. Upon thy belly shalt thou go, and dust shalt thou eat all the days of thy life. And I will put enmity between thee and the woman, and between thy seed and her seed; it shall bruise thy head, and thou shalt bruise his heel. (Genesis 3:14-15)

When the word curse is mentioned, we tend to look at the devil, Satan, demons and Lucifer. However, this may come as a shock to you; it's true, nonetheless. The first curse we have recorded in the scriptures came from God. Isn't this deep? Here's something more. The devil, Satan or Lucifer does not curse anything. The reason for this is because you cannot curse what you do not create. And, because the devil has not created anything he cannot curse anything. However, what the enemy can do is deceive you into cursing yourself. Here's what happened in today's true story. When the Lord dealt with Adam in his sinful decision to disobey Him, Adam blamed Eve. When Eve was confronted about the incident she blames the serpent. And, when the serpent was confronted he had no one to blame, so the judgment fell on him and with that judgment came a curse. What was that curse, you ask? Well as the story puts it, the snake would crawl on his belly and eat dust all the days of his life. God would place warfare between the seed of a woman and him. Wait, the problem in this story is women have eggs not seeds. However, there would be a woman, bearing a child whose seed would come from God; that would defeat this snake once and for all! At the Cross where Jesus died is the place where the battle took place. Here's the shout of the day: Adam and Eve missed it, the serpent messed it, and God fixed it!

Day 76: Yes, it's bad but It Could Have Been Worse

Unto the woman he said, "I will greatly multiply thy sorrow and thy conception; in sorrow thou shalt bring forth children; and thy desire shall be to thy husband, and he shall rule over thee." And unto Adam he said, "Because thou hast hearkened unto the voice of thy wife, and hast eaten of the tree, of which I commanded thee, thou shalt not eat of it. Cursed is the ground for thy sake. In sorrow shalt thou eat of it all the days of thy life. Thorns also and thistles shall it bring forth to thee. And thou shalt eat the herb of the field. In the sweat of thy face shalt thou eat bread, till thou return unto the ground; for out of it was't thou taken. For dust thou art, and unto dust shalt thou return." (Genesis 3:16-19)

Sin always brings judgment. Adam has to sweat and die. Eve has to live under her husband's rule, the earth will grow thorns and thistles and the snake will crawl and eat dust. Without any question this is bad; but keep in mind, it could have been worse! Take a moment to thank God for things being so well in your life, now; because it could always be worse.

Day 77: Good News, He Covered Me

Unto Adam also and to his wife did the Lord God make coats of skins, and clothed them. (Genesis 3:21)

What does God do with people who have done exactly what He said not to do? What does the Lord do with people who know better, but don't do better? What does God do with a person that has fallen and then had the nerve to blame others for their actions? Wait, here's the shout for the day: God curses the serpent, curses the earth, and He keeps the people! Are you rejoicing yet? You should be, and here's why. God should have cut Adam and Eve off and let them die. And then He could just start over. Only, He does not do that. God in His grace does not cut them off; He keeps them near. Why does God do this? Here's the answer you should hold on to for the rest of your life. This one principle flows through the Bible like a purple robe through a white quilt. God does not cut them off; He keeps them so they will always know His grace is their portion! In fact, here's the true story. God killed an animal, made coats of skin and covered them. God shed some blood and covered the people with what was sacrificed. The celebration of today is for every born-again believer in the Lord Jesus Christ who has ever done exactly what the Lord said not to do. For everyone who's been tricked by the devil and made some horrible mistakes; you have the right to shout aloud, "Good news, He covered me!"

Day 78: Killed Him in Cold Blood | The Story of Cain and Abel

And Cain talked with Abel his brother. And it came to pass, when they were in the field, that Cain rose up against Abel his brother, and slew him. And the Lord said unto Cain, "Where is Abel thy brother?" And he said, "I know not: Am I my brother's keeper?" (Genesis 4:8-9)

Murder! It's what took place in today's true story. You see, Adam and Eve continued onward because they were covered and they had children, two boys to be exact: Cain and Abel. One day, Cain and Abel went to make sacrifices to the Lord. God accepted Abel's offering, but He rejected Cain's. The reason the Lord accepted Abel's offering was simply because it was given to God first. Cain's offering was given to God from what he had left. When Cain noticed his offering had been rejected, he was so angry with his brother Abel, he walked smooth up to him and killed him in cold blood. So the first murder we have ever seen was not a drive by shooting, a lynching or a stabbing. It was more than likely strangulation. Cain probably grabbed his brother Abel around the throat and choked the life out of him. When scenes like this one surface, it is important to mention that sin has no boundary. It always takes you further than you want; making you stay longer than you plan to stay, and leaves you in a place you never expected to visit. Murder...killed him in cold blood.

Day 79: I'm Just Trying to Stay on Top | The Story of Noah and the Flood

And God said unto Noah, "The end of all flesh is come before me; for the earth is filled with violence through them; and, behold, I will destroy them with the earth." (Genesis 6:13)

This story has found its way into the annals of history around the world. It is the story of the great flood. The true story is deep and moving, to say the least. God is getting fed up with the radical rebellion of the people He created. So He decides to start over. He decides to bless a man whose name is Noah with a sermon to preach and some instructions to follow. The sermon is simple: It's gonna rain! That was Noah's first and final sermon. His instructions were much more complex. He was to build an ark and load it with all the animals, because God was going to destroy the earth with a flood by causing rain to fall for forty days and forty nights. It took Noah nearly seventy-five years to build his ship, because the vessel was massive. According to the true story given in scripture, it was five-hundred and ten feet long, fifty feet high and seventy-five feet wide. Critics ask, "How did Noah capture all of these animals and get them on the Ark?" The answer is simple. Animals came to Noah for refuge. In short, Noah did not have to capture them; they had enough sense to get on board because they could sense the rain was coming. If we could interview Noah right now; ask him why he stayed so faithful, and why did he stay the course? Noah would simply reply; "I'm just trying to stay on top!" In this light, staying on top is easy, just do what Noah did. Say what God told you to say and do what the Lord told you to do!

Day 80: Babbling Is Not Always A Waste | The Story of Babel

Therefore is the name of it called Babel; because the Lord did there confound the language of all the earth; and from thence did the Lord scatter them abroad upon the face of all the earth. (Genesis 11:9)

Television today is a modern day marvel. You can sit in your living room with a remote control in your hand and literally travel around the world. There's a show that comes on the Travel Channel called Around the World in a Day. It's an amazing broadcast that takes you on a journey of the seven continents and the beauty of each place. What was so awesome about the journey is it presents and highlights the cultures and languages shared by people around the world. In some of the video presentations it was as if the people being interviewed just babbled. From it, here's what can be deduced; babbling is not always a waste. In many instances, it is made by God for the inhabitants of the earth. Here's the true story: There was once a time the entire earth spoke the same language. Humankind put it in mind to build a tower extending from earth to heaven. The power of unity has so much strength, until God confused our languages at the Tower of Babel, as presented in the scriptures. It is where we borrow our word *Babble* from found in Genesis 11. In this vein, it is clear for us to see; babbling is not a waste, if what you are hearing can be understood. Here's a great devotional moment for you to consider. Have you ever walked into an Asian fish market or a Nigerian Restaurant and heard people speaking in their native languages? Did it sound like babbling to you? It was a language they could get a handle on and understand.

Day 81: Blessed To Be A Blessing | The Story of Abraham

Now the Lord had said unto Abram, "Get thee out of thy country, and from thy kindred, and from thy father's house, unto a land that I will shew thee. And I will make of thee a great nation. And I will bless thee, and make thy name great. And thou shalt be a blessing, and I will bless them that bless thee, and curse him that curseth thee. And in thee shall all families of the earth be blessed. (Genesis 12:1-3)

Here's the true story. His name is known around the world. Every continent, tribe and land has heard mention of his name. We should not be shocked or surprised by this because it was promised by the Lord in scripture. He is the patriarch of any religious faith expression in the world known for the worship and honor of the one God. What is his name, you ask? His name is Abraham. He was born in Ur of the Chaldeans in the land of Mesopotamia, in Babylon. The good news here is this: It's doesn't matter where you are from to God; it is where He is going to take you. God commands to leave the comfort of his country and kinsfolk to go to a land He will bless His people with and those people would come through him. Abraham grabs his wife, Sarah, to go to a place he has never been, with a map that doesn't exist because a God that he cannot see told him to do it. Talk about crazy faith! That is exactly what Abraham had. And, the praise in the passage is found in the promises God made Abraham. The Lord said, "And I will make of thee a great nation, and I will bless thee, and make thy name great; and thou shalt be a blessing." Without the life of Abraham, the story of Jesus would never come to pass. The blessing of Abraham carried with it the favor and person of our Messiah, Jesus Christ, Son of the living God!

Day 82: So You Think It's Funny, Huh | Sarah Laughs at God's Promise

Therefore, Sarah laughed within herself, saying, "After I am waxed old shall I have pleasure, my lord being old also?" And the Lord said unto Abraham, "Wherefore, did Sarah laugh. At the time appointed I will return unto thee, according to the time of life, and Sarah shall have a son." (Genesis 18:12-14)

God has to have a sense of humor. He often waits until things are humanly impossible and then says, "Now watch me work it out." He then probably chuckles to Himself and says "They aint seen nothing yet!" When God tells Abraham and Sarah they will have generations that number the grains of sand on the earth, they had no children. God waits until Sarah is ninety and Abraham is one-hundred before Isaac shows up! When the Lord sent the announcement the elderly couple would conceive and have a baby, Sarah laughed. The Lord heard it and said, "So you think its funny, hun?" He then lowered the boom on her. He said, "For nothing shall be impossible with God! And when your son is born, name him Isaac because you laughed." Here's the laugh of the day: Isaac means *He laughed* in Hebrew! Here's a solid query to ponder for a moment. Has God ever made you laugh before? What did He do? What happened? Keep your smile and tell your story. Our God is totally amazing!

Day 83: It's Only a Test | Abraham Tested with Isaac

And Abraham took the wood of the burnt offering and laid it upon Isaac his son. And he took the fire in his hand and a knife; and they went both of them together. And he said, "Behold the fire and the wood, but where is the lamb for a burnt offering?" (Genesis 22:6-7)

This is a story every believer should know and never forget. It's the story of Abraham being tested with his son Isaac. This story unfolds like a drama on a Hollywood screen. Abraham finally has the son he's always wanted. God calls and said, "Abe I need a favor." Abraham answered and said, "God, I'm here for you." The Lord instructs Abraham to take his son, his only son Isaac, to one the mountains of Moriah and sacrifice him there. Abe grabs his son, a few servants, the fire and the wood, and starts out on his journey. He travels for three days, waiting on the Lord to show him the right spot. They get to the foot of the mountain. Abraham tells his servants "Hold these mules. We will go worship and be right back." Abraham and Isaac start up the mountain. Isaac says, "Daddy, we have the fire and the wood, but where is the Lamb?" To which Abraham says, "God will provide Himself a Lamb." He places Isaac on the altar; and just before he takes his life, he sees a ram caught in the thicket. He sacrifices the ram and calls the name of that place, "Jehovah Jireh", meaning *The Lord will see to it.* What a story! Now here's the shout: Until God can have your Isaac, He will never really have you! Give God what you treasure and you will discover the treasures the Lord has for you that are in Him!

Day 84: Girl, You Know I Love You | Story of Isaac and Rebekah

And it came to pass, before he had done speaking, that, behold, Rebekah came out, who was born to Bethuel, son of Milcah, the wife of Nahor, Abraham's brother, with her pitcher upon her shoulder. And the damsel was very fair to look upon, a virgin, neither had any man known her: and she went down to the well, and filled her pitcher, and came up. (Genesis 24:15-16)

It was a father's dying wish his son find a good wife. A woman from within the ranks of his family to marry, and it happened like a love story only could. The servant of Abraham made an agreement with his master that he would make sure Isaac found a good woman to marry. This servant prayed. He said Lord, "Let the woman who gives me water to drink and my camel water to drink be the one." In other words, bring this man a woman who knows how to handle who he is and what he has, because the wrong woman in the family could mess everything up. At that very moment, Rachel pops up with a pitcher on her shoulder, gets the servant of Abraham water, and also waters his camel. When Isaac saw her, love was in the air. He knew she would be the mother of his children and the rest is history. Here's the principle: It's not hard to find what you really want, when you know exactly what you are looking for. The shout of this story: Through the lineage of Isaac and Rebekah comes our Savior and Redeemer, the Lord Jesus Christ. If Isaac and Rebekah don't connect Jesus will never be born. Thank you, Jesus for Holy Hookups, solid relational constructs, and men who can show up with a camel and say, "I'm looking for a wife. I know what I want; and I'm not leaving until I get what I came for!" Rachel was ready when Isaac showed up, and Isaac was ready when he met Rachel. It was a match made in heaven!

Day 85: They Are Not Identical Twins | Story of Esau and Jacob

And when her days to be delivered were fulfilled, behold, there were twins in her womb. And the first came out red, all over like a hairy garment; and they called his name Esau. And after that his brother came out, and his hand took hold on Esau's heel; and his name was called Jacob: and Isaac was threescore years old when she bare them. (Genesis 25:24-26)

The Sovereign rule of God bothers some people, because He does what He wants to do, when He wants to do it, to which He chooses to do it to, and there's nothing anyone can do about it. In this true story, God decides to bless Jacob before he is ever born. He is born holding the heel of his older brother Esau. Though they were twins, they were not identical in anyway. Jacob is a momma's boy and hangs around Rebecca, his mother. Esau is a hunter and is a father's dream. Esau is red and hairy. Jacob is smooth and handsome. God chose Jacob to be the descendent of the blessed nation of His people. Yet, he is a trickster, a deceiver, a supplanter. He swindled his brother out of his birth certificate for a bowl of stew. He tricked his father, with his mother's help, to snatch the blessing that should have gone to Esau for him. Jacob was a mess! But God decided to bless his mess and so it was. God used the mess of Jacob, whose name would be changed to Israel, to bear mighty sons that would construct the men that would become the cornerstone of the twelve tribes of Israel, today. Here's the moral of today's lesson: God blesses what He chooses to bless, and it's His decision.

Day 86: All in The Family / Story of Jacob's Children

There were the sons of Leah; Reuben, Jacob's firstborn, and Simeon. Also, there was Levi, Judah, Issachar, and Zebulun, the sons of Rachel; Joseph, and Benjamin: and the sons of Bilhah. Rachel's handmaid; Dan, and Naphtali: and the sons of Zilpah, Leah's handmaid, Gad, and Asher. These are the sons of Jacob, which were born to him in Padanaram. (Genesis 35:23-26)

All In The Family was a sitcom back in the late 70's early 80's, starring Carroll O'Connor as a man named, Archie Bunker. Yet when that phrase is used for the purpose of this study it carries much more meaning. You see, the lineage of Jesus Christ comes through this family tree. It is the lineage of Abraham, Isaac and Jacob. The family blessing of Jacob is most interesting. Jacob had two wives, Leah and Rachel. Leah was Laban's daughter and was described as having "soft eyes." That was a nice way of saying she was cross-eyed. Though she may not have been extremely attractive, she was fertile. She bore Reuben, Simeon, Levi, Judah, Issachar, and Zebulun. Rachel was Laban's daughter that Jacob waited fourteen years to get his hands on. Her beauty was stunning; however, she had difficulty having kids, but was blessed with two sons, Joseph and Benjamin. Jacob then had sons from Rachel's handmaid, Bilhah: Dan and Naphtali. As well, Jacob had sons from Leah's handmaid, Zilpah: Gad and Asher. Altogether, Jacob had twelve sons: eight sons from Leah's side; four sons from Rachel's side. To this day these sons are the nation of Israel. Without the seed of Abraham, the son of Isaac and the sons of Jacob, there is no Jesus Christ and no redemption from sin. Here's the shout: God chose the trickster like Jacob to help people like us come to know Him! He knew it was simply all in the family.

Day 87: I'm My Father's Favorite | Story of Joseph

Now Israel loved Joseph more than all his children, because he was the son of his old age, and he made him a coat of many colors. (Genesis 37:3)

Even though parents should not have favorites, they all do. Of course, a brilliant parent will never admit it, but the truth is there is always one child that grabs your heart. They tug at your soul and bring you just a little more joy than the others. In the story today, we find Jacob with the son of his old age, whose name is Joseph. Wait, Jacob has more children. But when it came to Joseph, the boy had a right to proclaim with vigor "I'm my father's favorite!" Jacob loved Joseph so much he did something for him he did not do for the others. He gave him a coat of many colors. It was a sign of his love and endearment. The problem is that when you are the favorite, it builds jealousy, envy, bitterness, and resentment from the others; and this family is no different. Joseph's brothers did not care for him at all. To make matters worse, Joseph was a dreamer. And, God revealed to him in two different dreams that he would be superior to his brothers. The dream was wonderful, but it is never wise to reveal your dream to someone who loves a nightmare. It is like throwing gasoline on an open fire. The blessing of this story is this: When people are cold, callous, and uncaring, do what Joseph learned to do. Wear your coat because it keeps you warm when your haters are absolutely cold.

Day 88: It's Not Punishment; It's Preparation | Story of Joseph in Egypt

And Joseph's master took him, and put him into the prison, a place where the king's prisoners were bound. And he was there in the prison, but the Lord was with Joseph, and showed him mercy, and gave him favor in the sight of the keeper of the prison. (Genesis 39:20-21)

There are times God allows moments of testing leading to a blessing, because it's not punishment; it is preparation. God knew Joseph would need supernatural strength to deal when facing his brothers who sold him into slavery. So He prepared him well. Joseph is lied about by Potiphar's wife; placed in prison on trumped-up charges, but because of his gift to interpret dreams, he winds up being second in command of the palace. When the famine in the land becomes dangerous, his brothers who wanted him dead need him. Joseph recognizes them; but he has been so blessed by the Lord that his brothers don't really know him. However, when they discover who he is, they know he could have them killed. Of course, Joseph is wounded by what they did, but his preparation made him see a bigger picture. It is then he declares to his brothers these words, "But as for you, ye thought evil against me. But God meant it unto good; to bring to pass, as it is this day; to save much people alive" (Gen. 50:20, KJV). In short, God let you try to hurt me, knowing I would bless you and my people the entire time! Here's a super portrait to peek at. Joseph reminds us of Jesus. He was a shepherd whose name means *Good Shepherd*. He was betrayed for thirty pieces of silver and from His sacrifice came the salvation of his people. Thank God for Joseph; but Jesus is on the way!

Day 89: If You Fail History, You Could Mess Up Your Destiny

Story of Israel in Egypt

Now there arose up a new king over Egypt, which knew not Joseph. And he said unto his people, "Behold, the people of the children of Israel are more and mightier than we. Come, let us deal wisely with them; lest they multiply, and it comes to pass, when there falleth out any war, they join also unto our enemies, and fight against us. And so get them up out of the land." (Exodus 1:8-10)

Someone once said, "If you do not learn your history, you are destined to repeat it." However, what is worse is the fact if you do not learn your history; you could destroy your destiny. It is what took place when Israel got to Egypt, and Joseph had passed away. You see, Joseph saved Egypt and blessed the entire nation, because he could interpret dreams. In the years of famine, the Egyptians had plenty because of the life and work of Joseph. Now, all of a sudden, there arises a Pharaoh who does not know of the works, toil, time, talent, and favor of Joseph. Pharaoh then starts to oppress the very nation that caused his land to be blessed. Here's a word to the wise, become familiar with your own history. If you don't know it, why should anyone else study it? And, if you don't share it, someone else will write it, and their view of it will not be yours. Pharaoh's ignorance will not only prove to be harmful, but later as this story unfolds you will discover that it will prove to be fatal, both he and his army will drown in the Red Sea. Here's a cultural query for you to consider. Have you become acquainted with your own history, yet? If you haven't, you should. Remember, if you fail history, you could mess up your destiny!

Day 90: Tell Him That I Am That I Am Said So

Story of Moses at the Burning Bush

Then Moses said to God, "If I come to Israel and say to them, 'The God of your fathers has sent me to you,' and they ask me, 'What is his name?' what shall I say to them?" God said to Moses, "I am who I am" and He said, "Say this to the people of Israel, 'I am has sent me to you.'" (Exodus 3:13-14)

This is the most quoted verse in the book of Exodus. Here's what it says, "I am that I am." But, did you know there is no "I" in Hebrew? The Hebrew alphabet is all consonants and reads from right to left and not left to right. "I am that I am" should really be spoken like this, "Ayeh! Ashar! Ayeh!" which translates like this: "He will be what He will be." The meaning suggests that whatever you need for God to be He can be just that, because He has the power to become it. Here's a great devotional moment for you to consider as you study. His Word today: What do you need for God to be for you…a doctor, a friend, a lawyer, a counselor, perhaps? Here's the shout of the day: God is big enough to be what you need Him to be, and He never has to stop being what He's always been to do it.

Day 91: Our God Is Greater | Story of the Plagues of Egypt

Exodus

Did you know the entire book of Exodus simply tells the story of how the Children made their way out of Egyptian captivity? It is really one magnificent story of the great exit of God's people from the oppression of the Egyptians. The blessing of this story is it is filled with theological duals between Jehovah, the one true and living God, and the gods of Egypt. In all ten plagues, the Egyptians were struck with; there was an Egyptian deity that was openly defeated by Jehovah. For example, when the water of the Nile became blood in Exodus 7, it was God's way of displaying His power over Osirus, the god of the Nile. When the plague of the frogs made their way through Egypt in Exodus 8, it was the Lord's way of openly showing His superiority over the Egyptian god Hegt, the goodness of fertility. And, when the livestock in Egypt died in Exodus 9, it was the Lord's way of displaying His sovereign will over the Egyptian god Apis, whose head is that of a bull. Yes, Egypt had deities that were claimed as gods; but there is only one God and His name is Jehovah! The one who is, was, and is to come. It was God's way of simply saying there is no other God besides me. Here's the great news of today's lesson: Your God has no equal! He is God and He alone is God. The moment our God has an equal, He will cease to be God. He cannot and will not cease to be God, because there is no other God with His power, presence, peace, protection, personality and passion for His people!

Day 92: I'm Coming out Of This | The Story of the Passover Lamb

For I will pass through the land of Egypt this night, and will smite all the firstborn in the land of Egypt. Both man and beast; and against all the gods of Egypt, I will execute judgment. 'I am the Lord.' And the blood shall be to you for a token upon the houses where ye are. And when I see the blood, I will pass over you, and the plague shall not be upon you to destroy you, when I smite the land of Egypt. (Exodus 12:12-13)

The word Exodus literally means "the exit." Thus, when you read the true stories printed on the pages of the text they are literally narratives that record how God delivered His people out of Egyptian captivity. A contemporary tagline for a book like this could better be translated, "I'm coming out of this!" The blessing of the story is that the people in bondage have no idea how God is going to do it. Many of the Israelites have been bound so long they don't even think freedom is a possibility. But, God always has a plan. During the tenth plague, the Lord tells His people to take a Lamb and roast it. They were instructed to take the blood of the Lamb and put it over the side posts and the doorposts of their homes. And, when the Lord would judge Egypt that night, any house with lamb's blood on it had a promise attached. God would Passover that house. The shout of this story is not the fact that the houses covered by the blood were protected. The celebration is the symbolism in the passage. A roasted lamb must go through the fire. In this, fire is a symbol of judgment. Thus, the Lamb is judged; not the people. Even more is the fact that in order to roast a lamb you had to put a long splint down his back and a short splint across his shoulders. If you stand the lamb upward, they had a Lamb on a cross, the whole time! You see, the only way to come out is through a Lamb on a Cross!

Day 93: Deliverance at A Dead End | The Story of Moses at the Red Sea

And Moses said unto the people, "Fear ye not, stand still, and see the salvation of the Lord, which he will shew to you to day. For the Egyptians whom ye have seen today, ye shall see them again no more forever. The Lord shall fight for you, and ye shall hold your peace. (Exodus 14:13-14)

Dead end streets can be so disparaging. You can't go forward, you can't travel to the left or the right, and in some instances you can't go backwards. A dead end can give you a feeling of hopelessness. This is how the Children of Israel felt right after they had been delivered from Egypt. God led them to a geographic cul-de-sac. It was a dead end! But the story isn't finished, just yet. In fact, it is far from over. God is about to show His people what deliverance at a dead end looks like. The Lord instructs Moses to make an announcement. Moses is told to tell the people "Don't be scared, relax; watch God work it out." Now here's the shout of the story. A strong east wind blows all nightlong and the wind that blows causes the waters of the Red Sea to stand up like decorative water walls and God's people walk across on dry ground. When the Egyptians come after them, they drown in the Red Sea. It is the greatest story of deliverance in the Bible, apart from the Cross of Calvary only. The blessing of this true story is the fact God tells His people He will be fighting for them. Question: Has God ever fought any battles for you? If He fought them, it means you have won them because God does not know how to lose

Day 94: It's The Law | The Story of the Ten Commandments

And God spake all these words, saying, "I am the Lord thy God, which have brought thee out of the land of Egypt, out of the house of bondage." (Exodus 20:1-2)

The truth revealed in this story is overwhelming. The people have been delivered from Egypt. But, there is a huge problem. There is still a lot of Egypt that remains in the people. God calls for a meeting with Moses on another mountain. Again, God appears by way of fire, to give Moses what we call the Ten Commandments or the Decalogue; laws that govern how we handle God and Laws that guide how we treat one another. All the while Moses is on the mountain, the children of Israel are in the valley having wild parties, getting drunk, and making idols that reminded them of back home in Egypt. What was given by God to Moses for people of faith still remains the raison d'être and cornerstone of our belief system to this day. The Law is good. In fact, the Law is flawless. However, the Law presents one huge problem. What is that you ask? No one can keep all of it. This makes all of us living on the planet lawbreakers of some sort. Just when we think we have all the law down, there is at least one Law we cannot keep. The good news about the Law is this: It came from God to us and God has a plan to save us from not keeping it.

Day 95: The Backside of Glory

The Story of Moses' Glimpse at the Promise Land

And it shall come to pass, while my glory passeth by, that I will put thee in a cleft of the rock. And will cover thee with my hand, while I pass by. And I will take away mine hand, and thou shalt see my back parts; but my face shall not be seen. (Exodus 33:22-23)

If you could ask God for one final wish before you died, what would it be? Perhaps, you would ask for a cure to horrible diseases. You may even ask the Lord to put an end to global poverty. It may even be in your heart to quiet earthquakes and cease all wars between nations. The fact of the matter is this; if you are like most people you would have a final request that would be something special right? Here's the true story expressed in this narrative. Moses is now an old man. It won't be long before he transitions from time and slips into eternity. He tells the Lord in no uncertain terms that, "Before I go I want to take a look at you. I've heard your voice, I've followed your instructions, I've seen what your hand can do, but I want to see you." God allows Moses to get a glimpse of the promise land. He takes Moses on another mountain, and puts him in a cleft of a rock. God then tells Moses, "And thou shalt see my back parts…" because no man can see His face and live. Now here's the blessing of what the Lord does, He shows Moses the backside of Glory! We are not really sure what Moses saw that day, but we do know this: When he descended from the mountain his face was glowing! So, if God gave you one final prayer answered; what would it be?

Day 96: Shout When I Tell You To | The Story of Joshua At Jericho

So the people shouted when the priests blew the trumpets. And it came to pass, when the people heard the sound of the trumpet and the people shouting, the wall fell down flat, so that the people went up into the city, every man straight before him, and they took the city. (Joshua 6:20)

The tension in the story is incredible, and here's why. Moses recently passed away; a new leader has been chosen by the Lord. His name is Joshua, a young noble inexperienced guy who has a tendency to be somewhat shy and timid. They are now in position to go into the Promised Land, but there is an overwhelming problem. The land promised to Israel is currently occupied. Imagine for a moment, God promised your great, great-grandfather a beautiful ranch with several houses on it for you and his descendants to inherit. You finally get the ranch, the rivers and lakes. They are gorgeous and the houses are splendid. But, there's people everywhere and smoke coming out every chimney. This is how Joshua feels when he gets to Jericho. The fight is on! God gives this new General the marching orders. The Lord said, "March once around the city, once a day for six days, and don't say anything. But, on the seventh day march seven times around the city, and on the seventh lap shout and sound the trumpets." In short, shout when I tell you to! Joshua and Israel follow these exact instructions and the walls of Jericho come falling down. People often ask, "How loud did they shout for the walls of a city to come falling down?" Here's the easy answer, it wasn't the volume of their shouts that caused the walls to fall. It was the fact they were faithful enough to do it! Stay faithful and watch the same God who blessed Israel at Jericho bless you.

Day 97: Misfits, Mercy and Might| Israel Ruled By Judges

Judges and officers shalt thou make thee in all thy gates, which the Lord thy God giveth thee, throughout thy tribes. That which is altogether just shalt thou follow, that thou mayest live, and inherit the land, which the Lord thy God giveth thee. (Deuteronomy 16:18-20)

If you haven't noticed it yet, God loves taking people who do not qualify and putting them in key positions. It is as if God says, "If I can win with them, you know I can win with anyone." The book of Judges pushes at its reader the salvation history of the Jew. During the shifts and scenes in this book, God ordered Judges to lead Israel. However, none of them really qualify. Ehud is a Moabite, Deborah is a woman with no real leadership experience, Othniel is no-good, Sampson keeps getting his haircut in the wrong barbershop, and Gideon is scared and doesn't want to fight. The entire group of them is nothing more than misfits in need of mercy and the Lord's might. Now here's the best news of the day. God intentionally chooses people like this to lead His people, then and now. The reason He does it is because you have to know that when the victory comes from, their efforts you'll have to know there was somebody bigger than they are on their side! Keep this in mind, if you're a misfit, you can't make it without His mercy, and if you have His mercy, you'll always have His might!

Day 98: Tall, Dark and Handsome | Story of King Saul

Then Samuel took a vial of oil and poured it upon his head, and kissed him, and said, "Is it not because the Lord hath anointed thee to be captain over his inheritance?" (1 Samuel 10:1)

With a description like this, one could have some of the single sisters looking for a handsome man waiting to be scooped up like a nice cup full of chocolate ice cream. After all we are an E-Harmony generation who looks for "likes" that become "followers", and "followers" who become "friends" and "friends" who become "dates" and "dates" who could possible become "a lifetime mate." However, the reference to "Tall, dark and handsome" does not come from an outline dating app. It comes from 1 Samuel, chapter ten where we are introduced to the man who will soon be the King. His name is Saul. According to the true story in the Bible, he's tall. It was said he was "head and shoulders" above the rest, literally. His skin was of a dark hue and his completion was solid. Saul's reign reached its peak when he defeated the Philistines by allowing a neophyte shepherd boy, David, to fight Goliath from Gath, and win. To do such back then would be equivalent to an NCAA football coach starting his towel boy at running back, only for him to run a touchdown and win the game! You see, sending David to the battlefield could have been the worst decision ever, if the young warrior had lost. But, thank God he won! That victory against a nation like the Philistines set Saul's leadership on a new all-time high!

Day 99: When The Oil Flows | Story of King David

And he sent and brought him in. Now he was ruddy, and withal of a beautiful countenance, and goodly to look at. And the Lord said, "Arise, anoint him, for this is he. Then Samuel took the horn of oil, and anointed him in the midst of his brethren, and the Spirit of the Lord came upon David from that day forward. So Samuel rose, and went to Ramah. (1 Samuel 16:12-13)

Remember this statement as you read bits and pieces of today's true story. Never judge a book by its cover. The people you overlook in life could become the very people you have to look up to before life is over. Such is the case in the life of King David. Here's how the story goes. Samuel has been sent by God to the house of Jesse to anoint one of his sons to be the next King. When Samuel arrives at the house of Jesse with the horn of oil used for consecrations like this one, the oil won't flow on any of his sons. Samuel then asks Jesse if he has any more sons. Jesse thinks for a moment and says "I have one more boy; it's not gonna be him, I don't think. He's keeping sheep in the field." Samuel says, "I will not sit down, until you bring me that son." The servants go to get David, and when he shows up he appears to be nothing more than a pretty boy kind of a guy. Samuel takes the horn of oil, and all of a sudden, the oil flows! Everyone there is shocked, because the sons they thought would be a great king is not the man the oil flowed onto. Here's the moral from today's lesson: You may not ever be man's choice. People may not ever choose you. But when you are God's choice, nothing else matters!

Day 100: The Bigger They Are The Harder They Fall | Story of David and Goliath

And it came to pass, when the Philistine arose, and came, and drew nigh, that David hastened, and then ran toward the army to meet the Philistine. And David put his hand in his bag, and took thence a stone, and flung it, and smote the Philistine. In his forehead, that the stone sunk; and he fell upon his face to the earth. (1 Samuel 17:48-49)

It has often been said the larger warrior should win. But there is also an epitaph that says "the bigger they are, the harder they fall." In this true story, it is exactly what happens. Israel is now faced-off against one of their repeated enemies, the Philistines. It was common then to have the nation's greatest warrior fight on the nation's behalf, thus sparing the lives of thousands of soldiers on the field of battle. The Philistines have a giant of a man fighting for them. His name is Goliath from Gath. He's nine feet, nine inches tall and talks plenty of trash. Israel doesn't have a representative, yet. Jesse sends David on a lunch-run to drop some sandwiches to his older brothers on the front line. When David sees this huge beast of a man intimidating the entire army of Israel, he says "Why are you all letting him frighten you? I'll fight him, because God is on our side." They rush David to King Saul and the King gives David his armor. But, David refuses. In short, David says, "I don't fight like that. I have had to fight a lion and bear in the woods to protect my father's sheep; all I needed is my sling shot." King Saul gives David the nod and he ends up on the battlefield, facing a man three times his size. He grabs five smooth stones, and says to the huge man "I come to you in the name of the Lord and the bigger they are, the harder they fall!" David takes the shot; hits Goliath right in the forehead, and he falls to his death. Here's the shout of today's lesson: Your enemy often only sees you. But do not see the fact that God is on your side!

Day 101: Don't Be Tardy For the Party | Story of David Becoming King

So all the elders of Israel came to the king to Hebron; and King David made a league with them in Hebron before the Lord: and they anointed David king over Israel. David was thirty years old when he began to reign, and he reigned forty years.(2 Samuel 5:3-4)

The story was told of a semi-inebriated man who raced up to the coronation of King Charles of England. Of course, he did not have the proper credentials, but he made his way into the crowd and blurted out loud enough for everyone to hear, "I have been planning to get here all day. I told myself no matter what happens to me today don't be tardy for the party!" There are some celebrations you cannot afford to miss. And, this party would have been one of them! In the passage listed, David is about to become King of United Israel; and it is a coronation fit for a King. The blessing of this story has its roots in fact that without David being King there would be no Jesus Christ and His throne. God organized and orchestrated the events of human history so David would be in the right place, at the right time, to do the right thing, so he could become King. With this in mind, from God's eternal throne in heaven to the annals of time on earth we discover that history is really HIS-story, because God is in complete control! Now here's the celebration news worth considering. There will be the coronation of another King whose reign will be from everlasting to everlasting! It will be by invitation only, and of course, the attire will be all-white fine linen. The shout that day will be a resounding mention of His wonderful name, Jesus! Jesus! Jesus! Like the fragrance after the rain! Jesus! Jesus! Jesus! Let all heaven and earth proclaim! Don't be tardy for that party!

Day 102: He's In the Batter's Box | Story of Solomon Becoming King

Even as I swear unto thee by the Lord God of Israel, saying, "Assuredly, Solomon thy son shall reign after me, and he shall sit upon my throne in my stead; even so, will I certainly do this day. (1 Kings 1:30)

The transcendent nature of God allows Him to be so far above us that time and space cannot contain all that He is. In a practical sense, to try to fit all of God into our finite human understanding would be like trying to place the waters from the Gulf of Mexico into a coffee cup from Starbucks. It's just way too much water for that cup to handle, right? With this in mind, God knows the end from the beginning. It is what is called the omniscience of God. He knows all there is to know about knowing and then He still knows some more. Here's the true story in this passage, while David was serving as King, God already had his replacement waiting in the batter's box. It would be his amazing son, Solomon. In the passage listed above, a mess breaks loose that would remind you of something from a Netflix series. Here's what happened. David got old and became too weak to be the king. All of a sudden, the guy whose name is Adonijah decided to make himself the new king. Yeah, that's right. He threw himself a party and everything. But, Solomon's mother, Bathsheba showed up at the king's bed and he remembered her and the son she bore for him, and on his deathbed declared Solomon would be the King. His reign would be one for the ages. He was the King who asked the Lord for wisdom. He would be the King who would build a house for the Lord and he would be the King who would change the face of the nation forever.

Day 103: But If Not | Story of Three Hebrew Boys in Babylon

If it be so, our God whom we serve is able to deliver us from the burning fiery furnace, and he will deliver us out of thine hand, O king. But if not, be it known unto thee, O king, we will not serve thy gods, nor worship the golden image, which thou hast set up. (Daniel 3:17-18)

We live in the age of compromise. Now, it is okay if a deal is on the table, and in order to make the deal work for all parties involved a little compromise may be needed and necessary. However, in many instances, it can be a horrible thing. For a parent to compromise their child's moral virtues is not acceptable. For a teacher to compromise the growth of a student and promote dishonesty is not good, at all. For a Christian to compromise the worship of our God because it is not the "popular" thing to do is absolutely not acceptable. The true story in the passage paints a portrait of three young Hebrew boys who have been taken captive by the Babylonians as a security measure against the Egyptians. King Nebuchadnezzar is now demanding the entire nation bow and worship a colossal statue he has erected for his glory. The band starts to play and every knee bows except the knees of Shadrack, Meshack and Abednego. They are threatened, but refused to compromise. In fact, here's what they say to the King, "Our God, whom we serve, is able to deliver us from the burning fiery furnace and He will deliver us out of thine hand, O King. But if not, be it known unto thee, O King, we will not serve thy gods." Have you ever found yourself in a place where compromise was easier? What did you do? Here's the prayer: Stand for Jesus just like He died for you!

Day 104: The Greatest Catnap Ever | Story of Daniel in the Lions' Den

Then the king commanded, and they brought Daniel, and cast him into the den of lions. Now the king spake and said unto Daniel, "Thy God whom thou servest continually, he will deliver thee." (Daniel 6:16)

A catnap is normally a quick little moment of sleep snatched by someone who just needs a little rest. Has it ever happened to you, before? You know, after a meal and you're sitting in your favorite spot and before you know it you're in another dimension. Well, here in today's true story this passage gives a catnap a brand new meaning. You see, Daniel has been thrown into the lion's den because he prayed to his God and would not cease. Now here's the irony of this true story: The King slept in a palace, guarded by men from his army, in a bed made for royalty and could not sleep a wink. Daniel slept in a huge cave with hungry carnivorous lions that needed to eat and his flesh would have been the perfect meal. Yet, Daniel took the mane of a lion and made a pillow out of it and slept all night long. Here's the shout, the next morning the King came to the lion's den and shouted "Daniel are you there?" Daniel answered "Yes King, I'm doing just fine!" Did you shout yet? If not, you should have. Daniel should have been dead, but the God we serve shut the jaws of a den of lions that could have eaten him alive. But, instead of being consumed by the king of the jungle, he was kept by another King whose name is Jesus! I've got a quick question. Ever had a catnap before? Instead of worrying about it, you went to sleep and God took care of it? Here's the blessing of this lesson: If He kept you before, He will do it again!

Day 105: Good News, God's Got Plans for You | Story of Israel in Babylon

"For I know the thoughts that I think toward you", saith the Lord, "thoughts of peace, and not of evil, to give you an expected end." (Jeremiah 29:11)

How would you feel if you discovered God loves you so much He would permit the worst of times in your life, but bless you like crazy while living in unfavorable conditions? Here in our true story today, Israel finds herself in Babylonian captivity. Yet, God has made His people a promise that He will not go back on. Here's what's deep. God is not going to take them out of Babylon just yet. In many instances, we make God look like the deity of all comfort. But this is not a true picture. There are times when God is the God of rough conditions and crazy circumstances. However, the shout of the day is that God's plans still prevail even in difficult times. Why is this, you ask? It is because God cannot lie. He not only tells the truth, He is the truth! So when God has plans for your life those plans are set for your life. In this passage, God tells Israel He has not forgotten the plans He has for them. And they are going to come to pass. However, for now the plan is bless them right where they are! So settle down, build some houses, have some children and remember the promise of the great plans that are coming your way!

Day 106: Tomorrow's News Today | Isaiah Foretells the Birth of Jesus

Therefore, the Lord himself shall give you a sign: Behold, a virgin shall conceive, and bear a son, and shall call his name Immanuel. (Isaiah 7:14)

On the New York Stock Exchange, they would call it insider trading. If you were playing the Texas Power Ball, it would make you a millionaire in about twenty minutes. If you were taking a Chemistry final exam on a college campus, it would make you the most loved person in the entire world by the students who are taking the class. What is it you ask? It is tomorrow's news day! In the Bible, news like this is called Prophecy. It is history written in advance. It is like knowing who will win the Super Bowl before the contest is ever played. It is like knowing when the storm will come ashore and knowing when to run from it or to stay put. The Prophet Isaiah brings forth some news to the people of God in this passage that is more than just prophecy. It is life changing news that is going to change the pace, face, and race of human history. A baby is going to be born. There's nothing really special about that, right? But here's the kicker; the mother of this child is still be a virgin. Now here's what's even more amazing about this prophecy. It was given about seven-hundred years before Christ was born. This is why the Wise Men were seeking Him, when He was born. They had been watching the stars for generations when the one star directed them where to find Him. The celebration for every Christian for news like this is that God made it clear. He would come the first time. Our shout is that He is going to be coming back soon!

Day 107: And With His Stripes | Isaiah Foretells the Death of Jesus

But he was wounded for our transgressions; he was bruised for our iniquities; the chastisement of our peace was upon him; and with his stripes we are healed. (Isaiah 53:5)

Isaiah not only tells us Christ would be born seven-hundred years before it would actually happen. But, he also declares Christ is going to die in the same manner. Now here's what's moving and life changing about this prophecy, Isaiah provides graphic detail as to what kind of death the Messiah would die. Here's what the passage says, "He would be wounded". A better translation of this word "wounded" would be pieced. He was also "bruised." This term means to be skinned alive! In the clearest since of the word, it would suggest the use of a Roman Centurion's whip filled with lead and bone. The word "stripes" refers to cuts that lacerate the skin wide enough to cause bleeding. My friend, all of this happened to Jesus the day He was crucified. Yet, Isaiah said it and declared it seven-hundred years before it came to pass. The real blessing of the text is that "healed" does not translate "mended from an illness", even though we often use this word in that way. However, the term "healed" means to rebuild or to restore something. It was used in the sense of construction to rebuild a bridge over land or water, designed to connect opposite sides, providing safe passage across. Get this; His stripes built a bridge that connects divinity and humanity; heaven and earth!

Day 108: Sometimes You Just Have To Wait | Israel Encouraged Waiting on the Lord

Wait on the Lord; be of good courage, and he shall strengthen thine heart. Wait, I say, on the Lord. (Psalms 27:14)

It is like using profane language, if you tell someone they have to do it. To impose it on anyone is to inflict harm and emotional hurt, usually. What is it you ask? It is waiting. The one thing this true story contains and explains for the Nation of Israel in particular and for people of the Christian faith in general is the benefit, bounty, and blessing of waiting. What are you to do when God does not give you any marching orders? You wait! What should you do when you do not know what to do? You wait! How do you function, when the road is dark, you have no map, and it seems like the rain is starting to pour? Here's what this passage exclaims: Wait! This Hebrew hymn holds within its confines the remedy for the righteous, as it relates to faithfully walking with the Lord, regularly. The answer requires faith to function, and it necessitates trust to activate. Wait! It is the Hebrew word "Quava" and it is in the stem that suggest this word is a used to reference the knees of a camel. You see, a camel spends most of its life on its knees, so they are tough and resilient. So, it is with those who are holding on, refusing to let go, who have come to grips with the fact that sometimes you just have to wait!

Day 109: The Wait Is Over | The Word Became Flesh

And the Word was made flesh, and dwelt among us, and we beheld his glory, the glory as of the only begotten of the Father, full of grace and truth. (John 1:14)

The city of Beaumont is the site for the county Fair each year. It will host and hold some of the best cuisines ever consumed on earth. It is filled with games, rides, a petting zoo and a rodeo. It is one of the largest attractions in the region, annually. Kids and grown-up's alike stand in line on opening day just waiting for the ribbon to be cut and an announcement to be made that lets Fair goers know the wait is over. People literally run through the gates because the wait is over. Here's true story that should bring joy to your heart and happiness to your soul. When it comes to our Messiah being born, our Savior being presented and our King being revealed so the world might know Him, the shout of the day is that the wait is over. Here's how John put it in his gospel. He said, "And the Word was made flesh and dwelt amongst us." The Greek here is fascinating; Theos, which is God who is the Logos (God's Word), became flesh (Humos or human). The remedy for human sin has been fixed in one person. He is heaven wrapped in a body. His blood will atone for every sin you ever committed! No more waiting! Run to Him!

Day 110: He's On a Mission | The Story of the Baptism of Jesus

And Jesus, when he was baptized, went up straightway out of the water. And, lo, the heavens were opened unto him, and he saw the Spirit of God descending like a dove, and lighting upon him. And lo, a voice from heaven, saying, "This is my beloved Son, in whom I am well pleased." (Matthew 3:16-17)

Tom Cruise is one of the nation's greatest actors. Though he stars in many films, he is most known for his movies bearing the title *Mission Impossible*. Tom Cruise does all of his own stunts. He does all of his own acting. And he knows that he is a man on a mission! If you think Tom Cruise was a man on a mission, just wait until you look at and analyze our master, Jesus Christ. Share in the gospel of Matthew. He is on a mission! He is about to turn the world upside down, so He can put it right side up. He is about to make a payment for sinners that only God himself could make. His mission is to redeem all of humankind. The great news of this passage is Jesus Christ is about to be baptized in water by John the Baptist. The purpose of His baptism is to express outwardly humble, radical, and faithful commitment to His Father who is in heaven. On the day Jesus was baptized, heaven opened like a scroll, and the presence of God descended in the shape of a dove. The voice of God was heard, saying, "This is my beloved Son in whom I am well pleased." This is a great devotional. Here's a question for you to consider. If Jesus was on a mission when he was on earth, what is your mission while you are here? Get to work, fulfill your purpose and be about your mission.

Day 111: A Rumble in the Jungle | The Temptation of Jesus

Then was Jesus led up of the Spirit into the wilderness to be tempted of the devil. (Matthew 4:1-11)

It was one of the greatest boxing matches of all time. It took place in the Democratic Republic of the Congo. The year was 1974! The two boxers that entered the ring that day were Muhammad Ali and George Foreman. It was a fight to the finish! Boxing promoter, Don King called this fight, "The Rumble in the Jungle!" Here's the true story you have to observe. The real rumble in the jungle happened in Matthew Chapter 4, when Jesus was tempted by the devil in the wilderness. Think of it this way, if the devil does not mind tempting Jesus, you know he does not mind attacking you. If you ask why this test was necessary; the answer would be simple and clear. Before there can be any public ministry done for the cause of the kingdom, there must first be some private victories over the flesh we must win. Jesus endured three major tests. Number one was the lust of the flesh. Number two was the lust of the eyes. And number three was the pride of life. Here's a great devotional. Question to ponder at a time like this. Have you ever experienced a rumble in your jungle? Here's an even better question to ponder. What makes your jungle rumble, right now? The good news is Jesus won his rumble in the jungle, so we as Christians could win ours. Oh, praise His name!

Day 112: The Man Can Just Flat Out Preach | The Sermon on the Mount

And seeing the multitudes, he went up into a mountain: and when he was set, his disciples came unto him, and he opened his mouth and taught them. (St. Matthew 5-7)

It's a comment you often hear by churchgoers who can appreciate a good sermon. Here's what you're usually hear. People who have gone to church and received God's word will often say "The man can just flat preach! " When it comes to the life and ministry of Jesus, one of the things He did on a regular basis, was preach. The word *Preach* in this sense comes from a Greek word, which means to share the good news. It is the good news about a Savior who is present to help sinners become saints and go free. In Matthew Chapters 5 and 6 we find the longest written sermon given by Jesus Christ in the Bible. This lesson is called the Sermon on the Mount. Jesus is sitting on a grassy slope with his disciples sitting around him. He begins with the Beatitudes. He then moves to the influence of every real Christian. In short, he started by telling us we were blessed because of what we are, who we are, and what we do. He then shifted to our influence. In that, we are like light and salt in the world we live in. Here's a good devotional question for you to ponder. What sermon taught by your pastor inspired you the most? Here's the prayer for you today: May the Lord bless those who are called by Him to speak into your life God's Word on a regular basis.

Day 113: We've Come up Short | The Feeding of the 5,000

And Jesus said, "Make the men sit down. Now there was much grass in the place. So the men sat down in number about five thousand. And Jesus took the loaves; and when he had given thanks, he distributed to the disciples, and the disciples to them that were set down; and likewise of the fishes as much as they would. (John 6:10-11)

Summer months in Southeast Texas can be hot. In fact, they can be downright, scorching. Not long ago while standing outside of a local community center, a group of kids we're waiting on snow cones. Initially, the ice was plentiful, and there was enough syrup to spare. After a time, the syrup was still full, but the ice started to run out. It was then a local community volunteer made a horrible announcement. She simply said, "We've come up short!" The feeding of the 5000 is a true story of what happens in the life of every believer from time to time. You see, during the story there is a need to feed 5000 people. But what they have in hand is not enough. Therefore, they have come up short. The shout of this passage is that our God specializes in helping, empowering, and strengthening people who have come up short. According to this story, Jesus took a little boy's lunch and started breaking it for the purpose of sharing it. And when he concluded, all 5000 men were filled. To make matters even greater, there were 12 baskets of bread left over. What a mighty God we serve! The blessing of the story is that when we've come up short God is still gracious, and can take our shortcomings to a place of merciful completion.

Day 114: Giving Him Something He Can Feel

A Woman with Issue of Blood Healed

And Jesus, immediately knowing in Himself that virtue had gone out of Him, turned Him about in the press, and asked, "Who touched my clothes?" And His disciples said unto him, "Thou sees the multitude thronging thee, and say thou, "Who touched me?" He looked round about to see her that had done this thing. (Mark 5:30-32)

As believers in Jesus Christ, we have a God that we can feel from time to time. The presence of God is evidenced in the human experience so much so that it affects the empirical senses of the human anatomy. With this in mind, have you ever felt God's presence before? Just to know the Lord is present can give you such an amazing sense of comfort and blessing. In short, we have a God that we can feel. However, it stands to reason, if we can feel our God, there has to be a point in which our God can feel us. In this true story listed in today's lesson, Jesus is touched by a woman who grabs His phylactery; (the hem of a Hebrew man's garment). When she touches His clothes, Jesus turns around in the crowd and says, "Who touched me?" The disciples reply that everyone is touching you in this huge crowd. But Jesus says someone special touched me! You see, the woman who was in the crowd was in desperate need of healing and she touched him. Her faith was so great, it caused the Lord to feel her presence in a way that Jesus said "Someone touched me." Here's a great devotional question to ask: When was the last time your faith made God feel it? Keep this in mind, if faith in God can move mountains, it can also move the heart of the Lord.

Day 115: Show Me Where You Put Him | Lazarus Resurrected

And when he thus had spoken, he cried with a loud voice, "Lazarus, come forth." And he that was dead came forth, bound hand and foot with grave-clothes: and his face was bound about with a napkin. Jesus saith unto them, "Loose him, and let him go." (John 11:43-44)

How would you respond, if you discovered your God was so awesome that even death could be reversed? What would it make you feel like to know your God is so amazing even death had to answer to him? Here in today's true story, we discover the life, death, and resurrection of a man whose name is Lazarus. He is the friend of Jesus; and he is a brother in the Christian movement who is valuable to our Lord. Mary and Martha are his sisters. They are all a wonderful part of the committed circle of kingdom workers for Jesus in the city of Bethany. Jesus discovers that Lazarus is sick, ill, and about to die. Instead of going to where he was, Jesus delayed for several days. The disciples come to grips with the fact Lazarus is not just sick; he is now dead! It is then Jesus begins His journey toward where he is located. When He arrives, both of the sisters of Lazarus come to the same conclusion "If you had been here, he would not have died!" It is then Jesus lowers the boom on them and says to them have you forgotten who I am? "I am the resurrection and the life, though he be dead yet shall he live! Show me where you put him." Jesus then spoke out to his friend. He said, "Lazarus, come forth!" And the man who was dead rose again! Here's the moral of today's story: Our God has no limit, no boundary, and no limitations. He has all power! As you journey through your day, keep this in mind.

Day 116: I'm Not Crazy; I Owe Him This | Mary and the Alabaster Box

Jesus was in Bethany, in the house of Simon the leper. As he sat at meat, a woman having an alabaster box of ointment of spikenard, very precious; approached Jesus. She broke the box, and poured it on his head. (Mark 14:3)

Have you ever reached a place in your life where you thought about how much you actually owe God? Imagine for a moment God sent you an invoice at the first of the month. And all the things He provided for you were marked on the billing statement. Things like breathing, sight, walking, talking, swallowing, touching, running, protection, provisions, peace, salvation, hope, and answered prayers, just to name a few things. How would you pay Him? Here in today's true story there is a woman present, whose name is Mary, the sister of Lazarus. She hears Jesus is in town and makes a decision to bless Him. She brings to a gathering of disciples an alabaster box filled with a very precious ointment called spikenard. She breaks the box and pours the expensive aromatic perfume all over Him. This is her way of saying you are my king, you are my hope, and I owe you this! You see, this fragrance was used by kings for different modes of coronation. It was also used to honor and pay great respect to those who would make great sacrifices. Mary knew because of His sacrifice she would be blessed. She also remembered that when her brother, Lazarus, was dead, Jesus fixed a problem for her she could not fix for herself. In short, she was not crazy for pouring her perfume on Jesus; she owed him a great deal. Here's a solid devotional question for you to think about today: How much do you owe God? If you are like most, you owe Him big-time. Here's how you pay Him back. Worship him with the life that he gives you every day!

Day 117: Three Strikes and You're In | Peter's Denial

And the second time the cock crowed. Peter called to mind the words Jesus said unto him, "Before the cock crows twice, thou shalt deny me thrice." And when he thought thereon, he wept. But go your way, tell his disciples and Peter that he goeth before you into Galilee: there shall ye see him, as He said unto you. (Mark 14:72 & 16:7)

The game of baseball is a worldwide sports phenomenon. People play the game of baseball all over the world. And, no matter where you find the game being played, a batter receives three strikes before they are called out. However, in today's true story, there is a man who is up to bat who receives three strikes and he is still counted in! His name is Peter, and he denies Jesus three times. He not only denies the Lord, but he curses and swears he does not know Jesus Christ. It is what many scholars' call Peter's denial. It is interesting to note that this same Peter would become one of the greatest apostles the church has ever known. Yet, he is the same man who would deny Jesus Christ publicly three times. The shouting news of today's lesson is that on Resurrection Sunday morning, an angel showed up at the tomb of Jesus, and told the women who were gathered there that He had risen! The angel then told the women at the tomb to have the men meet Jesus in Galilee, and to bring Peter with them! It was God's way of saying even though you've had three strikes; Peter, in my book you are still in! How many strikes have you had? How many times have you missed it here with some mercy for the moment and some grace for your day? God says, "You are still in!"

Day 118: You Thought You Knew Me, but there's more

Jesus' Transfiguration

And He was transfigured before them: and his face did shine as the sun, and his raiment was white as the light. And, behold, there appeared unto them Moses and Elias talking with him. (Matthew 17:2-3)

In the early part of the 20th century, Duke University did a study of theology, hoping to find conclusive, academic proof God could be figured out. In their study, they discovered every time they had God pinpointed, He would become something different in the next study. When they discovered God could be a healer, they also found out God could be a defender. When they found out God could be a savior, they also discovered He could be a friend. You'd say there was more to Him than they could ever discover. It was as if God took their study, and said "You thought you knew me, but there's more!" Here in today's true story, Jesus is being transfigured before the disciples' very eyes. By transfigured it means the deity within Him started to glow through the flesh that surrounded Him. What the disciples were about to come to grips with was that the God who lived on two legs while on earth was Jesus Christ. Jesus was, is, and remains God wrapped in a body! He is the incarnate word that walked, talked, preached, lived, healed, and died while on the earth. Here's the shout for the day: He not only died, but rose from the dead for our hope and salvation! Here's a great devotional. Here's a question for you to consider today: How well do you know Jesus? Never forget this; there's always more of Him to discover!

Day 119: They Trumped-Up the Charges | Jesus Falsely Accused

For many bared false witness against him, but their witness agreed not together. And there arose certain, and bare false witness against him, saying, "We heard Him say, 'I will destroy this temple that is made with hands, and within three days I will build another made without hands'." But neither so did their witness agree together. (Mark 14:56-59)

It is one thing to have someone lie about you. It is another to have someone under oath lie about your character. It is even worse to have those lies cause you to be put to death! This is what happened to Jesus Christ. After He was arrested on trumped-up charges, He was taken to an illegal court, and charged with crimes He never committed. To make matters worse, it took the court all nightlong to find two witnesses, whose lies matched. This was done because the law required the testimony of two people before a man could be put to death. So they lied on him all nightlong! Can you imagine listening to people lie about you after all you have done to simply help them? Can you imagine having something evil spoken against your character, when all you have ever done is good? The pain, agony, and hurt from this moment alone were devastating! Take a moment. Think about the worst lie anyone has ever shared about you. How did it make you feel? What did you do about it? The blessing of today's lesson is: Know that Jesus understood exactly how you felt.

Day 120: I Won't Let Hating You Kill Me | Jesus Forgives His Accusers

Then said Jesus, "Father, forgive them; for they know not what they do." And they parted his raiment, and cast lots. (Luke 23:34)

Okay, let's be transparent and blatantly honest for a moment. There are people that have hurt you deeply, and many times the only relief we have is to dislike them. It might be better to state it that we hate them. But, because we are Christians, we do not like using the word hate. Therefore, we soften the word hate and use the term dislike. We even go as far as redefining dislike so it does not appear that we hate. As we share this devotional moment together, it is important for you to realize hatred can be heavy. Hatred can make you bitter with people who have done absolutely nothing to you. It can also make you hard, evil, and callous. At this point, hating others can start to kill you. It can kill your joy. It can kill your hope. It can kill your happiness. It can murder you! While hanging on the cross, Jesus made a decision not to let the heaviness of hatred live in his heart! So He spoke these words, not only for the good of those who crucified him, but for the benefit of His own good; because hatred is always a heavy load to carry. Here's what He said, "Father forgive them, for they know not what they do." Here's a great question for our study today: Have you forgiven the people who have done the most damage in your life, yet? If you haven't forgiven them, let this moment of private study heal your heart of the dislike and hatred they have caused. In short, don't let hating them kill you!

Day 121: A Good Day to Die Hard | The Story of the Death of Jesus

Jesus, when he had cried again with a loud voice, yielded up the ghost. (Matthew 27:50)

It was what He was born to do. It was His purpose in life. It was His destiny, and it could not have been changed. It is why He was born. It is why He walked the dusty streets of Galilee. It is why He healed the man with the withered hand; and why He continued toward Jerusalem. It is why He was born in Bethlehem, conceived in Nazareth, and made His way to Jerusalem. It is why His blood would cleanse the sin of a world gone wayward. It is why He came! If you have missed the message of this entire devotional study, please, do not miss this. He was born to die! The sad and sanctifying news of today's lesson is He was nailed to a cross like a criminal. He was hung between two thieves. He was beaten all nightlong. He cried out "I'm thirsty." He cried out, "Father, forgive them, for they know not what they do." He cried out "Woman, behold your son." He cried out, "Today thou shalt be with me in paradise." He cried out "It is finished." He cried out, "Father into thy hands I commend my spirit." On this day the report from Jerusalem is one we should never ever forget. Here's the report: Jesus Christ died.

Day 122: How to Stage A Comeback | The Story of the Resurrection

"He is not here, for He has risen"; and he said. "Come; see the place where the Lord lain." (Matthew 28:6)

It is the true story of the greatest comeback in human history! In fact, there has never been a comeback like this one. Here is the root and fruit of today's true story. He is alive! Okay, let's spell it out here in this final devotional lesson of this book. To be dead is one thing; but to be alive three days later means something totally different! To be defeated in death is one thing; but to be resurrected and have all power is something victorious and totally different. My dear friend, Jesus Christ died for the sins of the world; but three days later the report from Jerusalem was the cross was vacant, the tomb was empty, and the throne in heaven was still occupied by a resident Father whose plan of redemption was so masterful it could save any sinner who would dare to simply believe! If there was ever a time when the church universal should shout triumphantly it is on a day like today! The saints of old would say it this way, "All hail the power of Jesus' name, let angels prostrate fall. Bring forth the royal diadem and crown Him *Lord of all!*" "Ride on King Jesus; ride on! Ride on King Jesus; ride on!" Here's our comeback shout for today and forever. He's alive! He's alive! HE'S ALIVE!